AF240902

From Head to Toe

SOCCER PHILOSOPHY

Max Milo Éditions, Paris, 2024
www.maxmilo.com
ISBN : 978-2-31501-270-1

GILLES VERVISCH

From Head to Toe

SOCCER PHILOSOPHY

Aknowledgements

Special thanks to Fabien "Bishop" Lévêque for the wealth of information in his master's thesis, Géopolitique du sport (Université de Provence, reference 2657, 2000).

Thanks to the sports professionals for their valuable information: Julie K., Isabelle L. and Marie-Ange A. Thanks to those who shared their passion for sport and soccer with me, Jean-Baptiste, Chiraze, Jean-Charles.

Thanks to Frédéric for the drawing.

Thanks to André for game nights.

Quote

"Know your ennemy[1]."

---

1. "Know thy enemy", *Rage against the machine,* Sony Music Entertainment Inc. 1992.

I. Would Thierry Henry have been Better off Playing Handball?
(Does the End Justify the Means?)

> "Men should know when they are defeated…[2]"
>
> Gladiator

FFF (French Federation of "the end justifies the means")

Noël Le Graët isn't bum Joe.

He is vice-president of the FFF or Fédération Française de Football, the authority that organizes and controls amateur and professional soccer in France. The FFF is an association under the law of 1901, whose purpose is to "defend the *moral* and material interests of soccer in France". We can well imagine that the material interests are to guarantee the means to practice the sport in the country at all levels. But

---

2. *"People should know when they're conquered."*

what are these moral interests? The question is all the more important as it is tantamount to asking the very body that is the authority on the subject what the *philosophy of soccer is*. One might think of banalities such as team spirit, respect for rules, referees and opponents, and so on. What's more, the FFF claims to carry out "the missions set out in the Code du sport", such as education, social integration, the fight against inequality, and other socialist-communist nonsense demanded by all those poor bastards. All the more so as the "federation" also aims to "respect the ethical rules of sport established by the National Olympic Committee[3]". But it seems that the "moral" interests of soccer are quite different from all this marshmallow of good feelings that are good for fags, when we're not fags! After the Ireland-France match, for example, the *aforementioned* vice-president of the *French Football* Federation was asked whether Thierry Henry's hand, which led to his team's goal, didn't spoil the joy of qualifying for the World Cup. Answer: "Not at all! We're thinking about qualifying first[4]." And as Pierre de Coubertin would say, "The most important thing is to win, even if you have to cheat!" In short, a very good way of finally understanding the "moral interests" of soccer in France. In this sense, it would seem that the "deontological rules of sport" followed by the FFF boil down to "the end justifies the means". The end is qualification for the

---

3. *Statuts FFF*, titre 1, section 1—objet.
4. *Le Télégramme*, November 19, 2009, interview by Dominique Morvan.

World Cup and, further down the line, the title of world champion; and the means is to cheat. Of course, *normally*, if it were just a question of playing soccer, we'd probably accept the basic rule that any wilful misconduct is disloyal and any cheating dishonest. But this is no laughing matter! It's not about playing soccer! It's not just about winning a soccer match! It's about… playing soccer and… winning a game of… soccer.

Nevertheless, the good vice-president simply says out loud what everyone else is thinking. And Thierry Henry must no doubt have wanted to please his sixty million fellow coaches by qualifying his team for the 2010 World Cup. But can we accept such a rule of conduct, especially when it comes to sport?

Should truth be preferred to lies?

Everyone agrees that you shouldn't lie—and some people think Thierry Henry should have admitted he'd done it. Lying is bad. Why is it wrong? We don't really know. Most people think they shouldn't lie, probably because they know they don't like being lied to; they suffer from it. As a result, it's assumed that "all truths are fair game". But as usual, a proverb allows us to avoid asking questions. If an SS man asks me to confess that I hid Jews, as in *Inglourious Basterds,* should I tell him the truth? The temptation is to say no. And yet, Kant asserts that under no circumstances should we lie, even if the circumstances seem to demand it.

I. Would Thierry Henry have been Better off Playing Handball?

Of course, this German philosopher would readily admit that the demand of the Nazi knocking on my door constitutes "illegitimate violence". *Illegitimate*, because there's no reason to want to attack an individual simply because he's a Jew; *violence*, because I'm under threat of repression that could go as far as death if I don't obey. Under these conditions, I may well feel compelled to tell the Nazi the truth, but on the other hand, I feel "absolutely obliged[5]" to lie. *Absolutely*, in other words, regardless of the situation, or rather, in accordance with a moral principle that seems to take precedence over all other considerations: that I must not be an accomplice to a criminal act. If I tell him where I've hidden the Jews he's looking for, I know very well what will happen to them, and it was precisely to save them that I hid them in the first place. Of course I'm frightened and may try to save my own skin, but I feel it would be cowardly to turn in these Jews.

But Kant maintains that what I am "absolutely obliged" to do, the duty that imposes itself on me and takes precedence over all other considerations, is, on the contrary, to tell the truth. An SS man asks me to tell him where I've hidden a Jewish family? In this case, as in all others, I must tell him the truth. Why should I? Of course, everyone will admit—and so will Kant—that in the situation in question, it seems far more humane, generous and even courageous

___

5. KANT (Emmanuel), "Sur un prétendu droit de mentir par humanité" (translated from German by Luc Ferry), in *Œuvres philosophiques*, Gallimard, "La Pléiade", 1986, t. III, p. 436.

to lie. But how to defend this argument? I know it's wrong to lie, but this is an exceptional situation! First of all, if it's right to lie in this situation, we can no longer say that lying is wrong in general. We can no longer say to children, "It's not nice to lie!" All we can teach them is that it depends on the case: sometimes it's good to lie, and sometimes it's bad. It all depends on the goal you're trying to achieve and the consequences that follow. And Thierry Henry might reply: "I don't see why I should have admitted my foul to the referee. You can always lie, depending on the situation". No, that's not the point! That's fine, but if you insist that lying is only a last resort in *truly* exceptional cases, then it's all the same, because we don't know what makes a case *truly* exceptional. So we'll always be able to say: "I don't usually cheat, but this is really exceptional" or "I couldn't have done it any other way!" In short, if we start accepting exceptions for all the good reasons we want, there's no point in laying down rules!

At the same time, if the morality so rigorously defended by Kant can justify handing Jews over to their executioner with such ease, then something must be wrong. That's why a certain Benjamin Constant defended the opposite position, which is more or less the same as saying "the end justifies the means". If the aim is to save Jews from certain death, it's all right to lie! Especially since we can sometimes lie to someone for their own good, like the doctor who lies to his patient to avoid ruining the little time he has left to live. On the other hand, you can also tell someone the truth in order to hurt them: "So, I hear you've got cancer? Ah… You didn't know? I'm very sorry to hear that." But when is lying justified? Benjamin Constant answers that truth only concerns "those who have a right to the truth. But no man has a right to the truth that harms others.[6]" So we can't say that lying is good or bad. The question is to know for what purpose or end one chooses to lie. If the end is good, so is the means. For example, we can certainly allow ourselves to commit an immoral act or one prohibited by law if we think it would be even worse to do nothing: this is the reaction of all those who call for civic disobedience, by destroying GMO fields, for example. This is because public health seems to them to be of greater interest than anything the law can say. Isn't it?

The player and the assassin

Of course, Thierry Henry didn't commit a foul in the name of public health, let alone to rescue Jews from the hands of the Nazis. It's simply to qualify the French team for a soccer World Cup. So it's not a "moral" act in the usual sense of the word. But it is what the FFF calls the "moral interest" of soccer, isn't it? Why should we care about anything else? We're not here to defend the widow and the orphan. We're here to see the French team win!

---

6. CONSTANT (Benjamin), *Des réactions politiques*, chap. VIII, Flammarion, "Champs", 1988, p. 137.

And that's how Noël Le Graët and others justify Thierry Henry's little wrist sprain: the national team's qualification is in France's best interest, so we can sacrifice the rules of soccer to it. "We're thinking of qualifying first". And "we" brings together a lot of people: firstly, the federation, which defends the material and moral interests of soccer in France. Then there are all the sponsors and other economic and media players who have an interest in France's participation in the World Cup to sell TV sets, shirts and advertising space. Politicians, too, must see this as a golden opportunity to enhance France's image in the eyes of other countries and boost the morale of its citizens. As a result, they start to consume again, boosting the country's economy. Finally, the French themselves are no doubt keen to follow their players at the World Cup, if only to indulge in one of those rare moments of collective enthusiasm. Thierry Henry must have done a lot of people good, including those who pretended to be scandalized. Let's be honest, who *really* would have preferred the French team to be eliminated with honors instead of qualifying? What would we have done this summer?

The French striker therefore acted as best he could. As he himself said in his defence: "I'm not the referee". How many players have thrown themselves heavily to the ground to win a free kick or penalty? How many players don't pull on their opponents' shirts, tackle them more or less regularly or raise their hands to the sky to signal a corner? It seems perfectly normal for players to defend their team's interests.

I. Would Thierry Henry have been Better off Playing Handball?

Secondly, it's up to the referee alone to apply the rules fairly. In a trial, you wouldn't ask a defendant to dig in his heels to help the jury convict him. On the contrary, we give him the right to play with all the elements he deems useful to his defense. He's even offered the advice of a lawyer to help him do so. Moreover, while all witnesses called to the stand must swear to tell the truth, the accused is under no such obligation. He is the only one who is allowed to lie if he thinks it will help him get off or reduce his sentence. After that, it's up to the judge or jury to evaluate each party's word and decide. And we wouldn't dream of making the accused responsible for the court's decision. *We can only blame the judge.* The accused's sole aim is to save his own skin. It's up to the judge to be concerned with justice. Each to his own role and each to his own objective, and it's no doubt the same in soccer: the aim of the players is to win, not to be fair—you'd know.

This spirit of soccer is also defended by Raymond Domenech. For example, when he talks about Zidane's headbutt in the 2006 World Cup final, he begins by saying: "In those moments, it would never have happened to me, this kind of absence from what we're doing. You can't do something like that[7]." At this point, you might think that the coach is blaming Zidane for getting carried away: "To forget what we're doing" would be to forget that we're playing a soccer match, all the more important because it's

7. January 28, 2010 interview with Charles Biétry for *L'équipe TV*.

a World Cup final. You're not out in the street or in your own backyard: everyone is watching, there's a referee and there are rules. The coach, for his part, would never have lost his temper in his playing days. But in fact, not at all! Raymond Domenech adds: "Even Sylvain, who can see that there's a problem, running with the ball, kicks it out to me to stop play. If the referee wants to stop, he stops! What I often criticize players for is not always having this idea: what do you have to do to win?" The problem with Zidane's headbutt wasn't that it was a violent act contrary to all the rules of soccer, it was that it jeopardized the French team's victory! Subsequently, the coach criticized Sylvain Wiltord for putting the ball into touch, when he should have kept running to distract the referees from Zidane's foul. In fact, his criticisms of Wiltord and Zidane stem from the same reason: they forgot that they had to do everything to win! Zidane shouldn't have head-butted Materazzi, not because it's wrong and contrary to the values of respect transmitted by soccer, but because it's an action that's detrimental to victory. And it's for the same reason that Wiltord was wrong to call a halt to play. As we said, the problem with the rules is the referee, and the problem with the players is winning. And Domenech must surely agree with Thierry Henry, firstly when he makes a handball, and secondly when he doesn't report himself to the referee. So, everyone seems to agree that a player doesn't first have to respect the rules. What is required is to act with the only thing that matters in mind: winning.

I. Would Thierry Henry have been Better off Playing Handball?

An action is not good or bad because it goes against the rules, but only insofar as it is useful or harmful to victory. The end justifies the means, and in this sense, the spirit of soccer is essentially *Machiavellian*.

Has Thierry Henry read Machiavelli?

Lilian Thuram must have read Machiavelli, given that he wears glasses, which is not the case for Thierry Henry. However, the French striker does seem to have read Machiavelli. Machiavelli? Machiavelli was the author of the "ends justify the means" rule, even if the exact phrase is not to be found in his writings. That said, we do come across a phrase like: "In the actions of all men [...], the end is considered. Let a prince, therefore, take steps to conquer and maintain the State: the means will always be judged honourable and praised by everyone[8]". For most people, Machiavelli's name has remained associated with the adjective "Machiavellian": a wicked person who uses all his intelligence to do evil. The term "Machiavellian plan" is virtually synonymous with "diabolical". But that's not to say that Machiavelli himself did anything nefarious. If his name has remained associated with the image of the cunning villain, it's because, in *The Prince*, he sets out to explain to those who will listen how to conquer

---

8. MACHIAVELLI (Nicolaus), *The Prince*, chap. XVIII, (trans. from Italian by Yves Lévy), GF-Flammarion, 1992, p. 143.

and retain political power. And in such matters, it's best not to be sentimental, whatever the situation. Although Machiavelli's advice was aimed at the rulers of his time, the princes and monarchs of the 16th century, it applies to all those who aspire to power, including those in modern democracies. He doesn't pretend to write a political treatise on the ideal city, claiming to be interested in the poor, to affirm that "all men are equal", that we must think "of the most fragile among us", my ass on the chest of drawers, and so on. It doesn't matter whether the prince or the candidate in power is good or bad, left or right, green or fascist. The main thing is to know how to conquer power and keep it; to get re-elected. And if that's your ambition, there's no need to get fancy. There are circumstances in which you'll have to be nasty, others in which you'll have to lie, be hypocritical, and so on. For example, the politician or "prince" must know that "it is necessary to have the friendship of the people; otherwise, in adversity, there is no remedy.[9]" So, no matter how much you're attacked or hated by your political opponents, or even the "friends" of your own party, you'll always come out on top if you've got public opinion, the polls and the voters on your side. And how can a political candidate or leader win the love of "the people" or the electorate? According to Machiavelli, it's enough if "the measures he takes maintain the popular

---

9. *Ibid*, chap. IX, p. 107.

ardor[10]". Indeed, what could be more effective than a great sporting adventure to sustain popular ardor? Experience has shown that a World Cup title is enough to get you re-elected president, whatever else you do, because people will always think that there must be some connection between the performance of their national team and the political skills of their leaders.

It all sounds quite immoral, but is intended to be rather realistic. We don't pretend to teach politicians how to govern well or "do good". That's up to you—"some have tried, but ran into problems", like Jospin or Bérégovoy. However, it's not a question of saying that we *should* do evil or that we should be mean. It's simply that we have to admit that politics, or at least political conquest, has nothing to do with morality. When you want to lead, you shouldn't ask yourself what's right or wrong, but what leads effectively to power. In the same way, if, like Thierry Henry, you want your team to win or qualify for the World Cup, you shouldn't try to play by the rules at all costs. Of course, cheating isn't very pretty, nor very *fair play*, but you have to know what you want: who wants the end, wants the means. Of course, we'd have preferred to have qualified on a regular basis, if we could have, and Thierry Henry was the first to do so! But the main thing is saved, isn't it? "We're thinking about qualifying first."

---

10. *Ibid*, chap. IX, p. 107.

Performance rather than victory

And yet, if it's not in an international professional soccer match that you have to respect the rules, it's hard to see where you could do so. Admittedly, the "professional" is, compared to the amateur, the one who is paid to win. Nevertheless, we also have the right to expect him to practice his activity with "professionalism", in other words, far better than the amateur. When we speak of "high-level" sport, we might think that we're talking about a high level of training, practice and mastery, compared to the Sunday footballer. But apparently it means "high level of cheating". Sportsmanship is good for amateurs, but when you're a real sportsman, you have other priorities! Victory! To that extent, you can cheat in any way you like, even to the point of doping. But we want to say: what do you win? A soccer match or competition? The problem is that in "winning at soccer", there's "winning", of course, but there's also "at soccer". And everyone seems to have forgotten that.

What is soccer? It's a team sport based on the principle of "kicking a leather ball into the opponent's goal with any part of the body *except the hands* (and arms)[11]." It's easy to imagine, then, that there are few or no rules, so that the most violent team wins, as was the case in soule, the ancestor of all these ball games. If we want to engage in

---

11. Dauven (Jean), *Technique des sports*, PUF, "Que sais-je?", 1969, p. 94.

I. Would Thierry Henry have been Better off Playing Handball?

a purely physical confrontation, we can reduce the rules: one ball in the middle—so that both sides can hope to win—and the first to send it into the opponent's goal wins. Victory goes to those with the best physical qualities: the fastest, the strongest, even the most violent. When "no holds barred", there's no quarter given! But in soccer, someone decided to add the annoying rule that you can play the ball with any part of your body, *except your hands*. Why "except the hands"? And why not? In fact, there's another sport directly modelled on soccer that can be played by those who prefer to play with their hands: handball, where the rule is reversed: instead of playing only with your feet, you use only your hands.

So, if you've won in a *team sport by scoring with your hand,* you may well have won a handball match, but you haven't played soccer! So it's not just a question of cheating. As we've seen, handball is essential to soccer. This means that it's the defining rule of the sport, and the one by which soccer is played *rather* than any other game. All team sports are somewhat similar: there are always goals, opposing sides and so on. And when it comes down to it, the number of players, the size of the pitch or the size of the goals doesn't really matter. In fact, depending on the material possibilities, a soccer match can be played on a much smaller pitch than in an official stadium, with two or four players and sweaters on the ground to mark the goals. What's essential, what justifies playing soccer, is that you use your feet above all, and possibly your head too. Soccer is played from head to toe, without using your hands. But the problem is that, with spectator sport and the political, economic and social stakes involved, the sport itself is less important than winning. It doesn't matter whether you play soccer or handball, you've got to take part in the World Cup. And if you manage to qualify for the World Cup after winning, as you did in handball, it doesn't matter! What counts is having a team at the World Cup; it's about ensuring France's presence in the most watched international competition. Basically, we'd probably have preferred handball to be the most popular sport in the world. But it's soccer. The problem is that a player who starts cheating to qualify his team completely forgets the essence of the sport, so much so that he could be considered to have no business being on the pitch. Those who "think first about qualifying" are very much mistaken. Because a player has to think about the rules first. Otherwise, he changes his game. Or they don't play at all! "The end justifies the means?" But all these good people have reversed the ends and the means! A sportsman's end and purpose is to play sport, to develop all the physical and mental qualities that it tests. As for the goal, it's just an excuse to motivate yourself. And if you don't feel up to confronting the rules and opponents that are the very essence of the game, all you have to do is something else.

"It's a perfectly natural thing to desire to acquire," admits Machiavelli. To acquire, and so to speak, to conquer and win. "And always, when men *who can* do so do, they will

I. Would Thierry Henry have been Better off Playing Handball?

be praised, not blamed. But *when they cannot*, and want to do it by all means, there is error and blame[12]." Men must know when they are defeated, and admit defeat. This is how sport can teach us the spirit of democracy.

12. *Ibid*, chap. III, p. 79.

II. Why Say, "We Won," When we weren't Even on the Field?
(Is Soccer the Opium of the People?)

"It's the world that's been placed before your eyes to prevent you from seeing the truth.
- What truth?
- That you're a slave!"

Matrix

They won, I lost

1998 World Cup. I didn't see the quarter-final penalty shoot-out in which France beat Italy. The famous moment when Luigi di Biagio hit the crossbar before collapsing to the ground on his knees. The famous moment, seen a thousand times over in *Les yeux dans les Bleus*, when Patrick Vieira and Franck Lebœuf, seated near the bench, asked each other premonitory questions:

"Is that the last shooter there? Is that the last shooter?

— If he scores and the other misses, have we won?"

It's true that it's easy to get caught up in the emotion of seeing these images again. That said, it will always be different from the way I experienced the event on the day itself. For me, it was the day I was flunked at the agrég de philo exam, the first time I took it—and therefore not the last. I was still waiting for the results when the game started, and then I realized I'd been turned down. A member of the jury even told me that I'd been the worst of all the candidates at the oral. What's more, I'd just been dumped by the girl I'd been with for over a year—a record!—and who'd probably found someone else in the States. So I felt like a piece of shit wandering the streets. I was trying to understand why I'd worked for a year for nothing, and I wondered if I'd have the strength to start all over again. By the time I got to my brother's place, it was already penalty shoot-out time, and it was probably because he was watching the game in front of his TV screen that he didn't hear me ring the bell. The street was invaded by the sound of all the TVs coming out of all the windows in all the buildings. I could hear people's cries of joy and disappointment. Obviously, some apartments were occupied by Italians. It was a strange atmosphere. From time to time, some people would stick their heads out of the window to shout the score and share their enthusiasm with their neighbors. Then, a louder and longer shout told me it was all over.

"We've won! We've won!"

But who is "we"? Them? And what exactly did we win?

Understandably, my feelings were very mixed. Of course, by the time of the semi-final, I'd already forgotten the disappointment of my personal history. And after the big final against Brazil, like everyone else on the evening of July 12, I marched down the street, singing and feeling with deep, heartfelt joy, "We've won!" Yet I was still dumped, sulked, failed and lost.

So you might ask: who cares about his story? Well, maybe it's everyone's story, after all. Why on earth did I find myself marching with all these people I didn't know, to celebrate a victory that wasn't mine? We shared our soccer team's victory "all together", as if France had just been liberated from the Nazis. No doubt we were looking forward to a happy tomorrow. Yet the next morning, I didn't wake up thinking "we've won", but "what am I going to do now?

And how long did that World Cup victory help you forget yourself?

Sport is just sport

From a grammatical point of view, "on" refers to everyone and no one. It's "someone". So you can say "we won" without any mistake, if it means "someone won". But we know that in everyday language, "we" means "us". This expresses the idea of a group, or even a community to which I feel I belong. There are couples like that who get on everyone's nerves. Whether it's him or her, they're

II. Why Say, "We Won," When we weren't Even on the Field?

always saying "we" or "us"; unable to think for themselves, always glued to each other, making out.

"But *you*? You there! What do you think?

— Well, I don't know… honey, what do we think?"

So why is it that when eleven guys you don't know from lips or teeth win a sporting event, there are tens of millions of others who think they've won something[13]? It's understandable that the players on the pitch might say "we've won" or, what amounts to the same thing, "we're world champions". And their team-mates on the bench can say it too: even if they didn't play at all, the members of the French team officially selected attended training sessions with the others, shared their rooms, their retirement, etc. Their presence must certainly have been a major factor in the success of the tournament. Their presence must certainly have had some effect on the morale and performance of their fellow players and room-mates. But apart from these players and the *staff*, who can claim this victory?

In most sports, when the French win, we're happy *for them*. We can even be proud of them, because they offer a beautiful image of the country to which we belong and allow it to exist outside its borders. For example, who knows São Tomé and Príncipe? No one does. And yet, it's a

---

13. Just over 20 million viewers for the 1998 France-Brazil World Cup final, a third of the French population. And again, over 22 million viewers for the 2006 World Cup, for the France-Portugal semi-final and the France-Italy final. Audiences reached almost 80% market share.

country. But that's probably because, unlike the islands of Trinidad and Tobago, a former colony of the same name, we haven't been able to find anyone who can run the 100-meter dash in under 20 seconds.

And if we're proud of the athletes who represent our country, we know that sport is only *one part of* a society's activities, and it's as such that we consider it, especially when it comes to top-level sport. In this case, only a small category of athletes are concerned, the others being mere spectators, even if they practice the same sport as amateurs. So we can congratulate the French handball team on winning the world championship. And we're probably right not to make too much of it: this victory means that France has a good framework for the high-level sport of handball, even if nobody in the population plays it. It's a bit like what happens in skiing: we wait for the French team's "medal chances", we even demand that they win some, even though few people practice this sport[14]. Bravo! "We've" won a *handball* competition, nothing more, nothing less. And if the French team had lost, it would have been a non-event. In fact, it's only when sportsmen and women reach the final phase of a competition that we start talking about them. A tennis player reaches the semi-finals of the US Open, and France2 offers to "shake up its programming" to broadcast the match.

---

14. Insee, 2007: 138,146 members of the French Ski Federation. Despite the exaggerated media coverage, only 9% of French people go on winter sports outings (Insee, 2004).

And it took Sébastien Loeb at least five or six World Rally Championship titles to get people talking about him. Those who like handball, basketball, golf or pétanque may well regret having to subscribe to pay-TV channels to follow their favorite sport. At the same time, sport is just one of many activities that fall within the realm of leisure. Leisure itself is the set of activities with which we fill our free time. In other words, it's the set of activities that members of a society can engage in, insofar as they are strictly *useless* to that society and depend solely on individual tastes and preferences. Of course, the practice of a sport can have an educational function. But when it comes to top-level sport, where you're just a spectator, isn't it just another leisure activity?

Those who complain that they don't see enough 10-meter pistol shooting on TV need to get used to the fact[15]. Top-level sport is just one *part of* the world of sport *spectacle*, itself just one *part* of the whole of leisure activities, which are themselves just one *part* of social life—the most useless and subjective part, in fact. So why should I be concerned by the victory of the fine team of eleven?

---

15. Don't laugh too soon! The French Shooting Federation has 132,537 members. So there's no reason why there should be more skiing than 10-meter pistol shooting!

Canal+ is the opium of the people

Of course, I know that soccer is much more popular than 10-meter shooting. But why soccer rather than any other sport? It's hard to say. Some physical education professionals think it's the easiest sport to play. Firstly, because a child can kick a ball very quickly, whereas it's harder to catch a ball with the hands. Secondly, soccer can be played anywhere: on the lawn of a public garden, in a vacant lot or at the foot of a building; bottles, a sweater or old socks to mark out the goals and you've got your soccer pitch. It's a different kettle of fish when it comes to improvising a rugby, volleyball or tennis pitch. And yet, it's not clear that the popularity of soccer has much to do with the fact that people play it themselves. After all, it's just as easy to improvise a boules pitch without the daily nuisance of pétanque competitions. Admittedly, soccer is by far the sport with the largest number of official players, with over two million licensees[16]. But it's obvious that not all the 22 million spectators who shouted "we've won" after the 1998 World Cup final play soccer. What's more, the popularity of a sport as a *spectacle* is not necessarily related to the number of people who play it. Indeed, while soccer is the most widely televised sport, rugby comes in second

---

16. 2,320,625 soccer licensees, ahead of tennis with 1,094,593 and judo with 550,382 (Insee, 2007).

place[17]. However, the "oval ball", which has become so familiar through the Top 14, the Six Nations Tournament and the World Cup, has ten times fewer licence-holders than soccer, and fewer than horse-riding, basketball, handball, golf and even pétanque[18]. And yet, these sports, especially pétanque, are rarely broadcast on the major TV channels. At the same time, it must be boring to watch. In any case, we'll have to admit that the audience for a *spectator* sport isn't necessarily linked to the popularity of the sport itself. I even know people who don't like to watch their sport on TV, for the good reason that they're only interested in playing it. What's more, drinking 8.6 and other Heineken beers has never been known to develop an athlete's physical faculties. So those who watch don't always have the same dispositions or motivations as those who play. And while players may drink their way to victory during a third half, they are rarely drunk from the start of the match, which is not always the case for supporters and other (TV) spectators.

But if soccer is on TV every day, if every newsflash in every media outlet gives the results of National League matches as regularly as the weather forecast, it's not, first

---

17. According to the CSA, for example, 507 hours of soccer programs were broadcast in 2006, ahead of 160 hours for rugby.
18. 553,560 members of the Fédération française d'équitation, 457,121 for basketball, 383,949 for golf, 367,047 for handball and 362,867 for the Fédération française de pétanque et jeu provençal! That's far more than the number of rugby licensees, who number just 285,376 (Insee, 2007).

and foremost, because it's the national sport played by every French kid in every neighborhood; it's because Canal+ bought the rights to broadcast the French Championship in 1984. Before that, there were less than thirty matches a year; since then, there have been at least forty… a week!

It would be hard not to mention all the economic interests at stake in the organization of the soccer *spectacle*: those of the federations, who receive money by selling the broadcasting rights to various channels such as Canal+ or TF1; those of the same channels, who thus increase their ratings and can sell the advertising space offered during the matches at a premium, like TF1. And these advertisers themselves gain customers thanks to their advertising, in the form of commercials or sponsorship. Finally, there are the clubs to whom the federations redistribute part of the money made from the sale of TV rights. Without going into too much detail[19], it's easy to see why all these groups can justifiably exclaim, "We've won!" But what have viewers gained?

He won the right to buy Heineken or Coca-Cola, "official partner of the French team", to share a good match "avé' les

---

19. For those who still want the details, here they are: Canal+ pays 600 million euros per season to the French Football League (delegated by the FFF) for the rights to broadcast the French Championship. As for World Cup broadcasting rights, they cost a total of 84 million euros in 1998, 746 million in 2002 and 970 million in 2006; and all this is for FIFA! In France, TF1 bought the rights to the main matches of the 2006 World Cup for 100 million euros, and those of 2010 for 120 million. As a result, TF1 sold a 30-second advert for the 2006 final for 284,500 euros.

copaings" ("with the guys"). Then, a good night's sleep to be fresh and ready the next morning to go to work and make money for his company: BNP Paribas, Renault, Groupama, Bouygues, etc. And what do we do with the money we've earned? We spend it on the weekend to buy everything we "saw on TV" during the match: the French team's Adidas shoes, Ribéry's Nike cap, the Orange package, partner of Canal+; and also, the products of the advertisers who invested so much in the match ads: the BMW that "creates joy" and a Groupama insurance policy. "Merci Cerise!" In short, we spend the week working to produce goods for the companies that sell them back to us on our days off. Don't you feel like you've been swindled by history?

You think that's cynical?

Sentimental crowd

Of course, if companies and the media invest so much money in soccer, it's undoubtedly to meet viewers' expectations. We're not inventing a feeling, and it would certainly have been much harder to sell us the World 10-meter pistol shooting championship. You feel really happy when your team wins a competition. You follow your team's progress with enthusiasm, and the simple fact of reliving the high points "with your eyes on the Blues" is enough to awaken the emotions you've experienced. So there's definitely an aspiration that drives us, and which the *spectacle* of soccer seems to respond to. But what is it?

I'd tell you about 18th-century English philosophers like Hume or Shaftesbury. But I have a feeling that won't ring a bell. On the other hand, we can remember Alain Souchon's song, *Foule sentimentale*. You know what it's like to say of someone "he's a great sentimentalist". It means that you indulge in feelings; that you enjoy experiencing them, even if they're rather painful, like sadness or nostalgia. At least we feel something and feel alive. In fact, this emotional faculty is undoubtedly what essentially characterizes life. Animals feel sensations when touched, stroked or hit, unlike stones or corpses, from which all organs can be removed without apology, as TF1's *Les experts* demonstrate so well on evenings when the series isn't cancelled due to a match. But without even being touched, living beings also feel things inside them that set them in motion and drive them to act, starting with hunger, thirst or the sexual instinct, all of which are needs that must be satisfied, insofar as they are experienced as lacks that we therefore seek to fill. And while lack in animals can be reduced to natural needs, in humans it takes the form of desire. As the song says, "on a soif d'*idéal*" ("we crave the *ideal*"): the lack felt by man and which drives him to act is also of an intellectual nature; it belongs to the realm of *ideas*. When we read, educate ourselves, take an interest in history or art exhibitions, we're not nurturing our bodies. These are merely "spiritual nourishments" designed to satisfy the needs of the spirit, which we then call "aspirations". All these desires, and the activities to which they lead us, have a tendency to elevate us, enabling us to move beyond the satisfaction of natural, material needs. These aspirations drive us to act to realize our ideals. Thus, scientific progress, artistic creation and political commitment undoubtedly owe a great deal to these desires. And if man had always been content with what he had, he would still be living in caves and would probably not have transformed the world in his own image.

Man is therefore a great sentimentalist, insofar as he likes to experience feelings that are all the stronger for their spiritual nature. Doesn't the pleasure of watching a film or listening to music stem from all the feelings it inspires? And can we deny that this pleasure has nothing physical about it? But above all, Souchon's song tells us that we are a sentimental *crowd*. In other words, our feelings are all the stronger when shared with others. "Reduce a man to solitude, and he will lose all joy[20]", says the aforementioned Hume, of whom I'll have finished speaking. It's hardly necessary to justify this statement, which will speak to everyone. Why, on the big night of a final, do we seek out a bar broadcasting the match or giant screens set up in public squares, if not to share our emotions in front of the same spectacle? Why else invite friends over to watch the game at home? When

---

20. HUME (David), *Enquiry into the Principles of Morals*, Section V, Part 2, (trans. by P. Baranger and P. Saltel), GF-Flammarion, 1991, p. 129.

you're on your own, the highlights just don't have the same flavor, or the same force. In the end, it's not the events themselves that are powerful, it's the feelings they inspire, which are all the more intense the more you can share them. Why is this? It's hard to say. The same Hume borrows the image of mirrors to try and describe this rather indefinable communicative enthusiasm: "The minds of men are mirrors to each other [...] because each reflects the emotions of the others[21]". This is how Indiana Jones lights the Egyptian temple in *Raiders of the Lost Ark*. As this is an underground cave built in antiquity, it is illuminated by a system of mirrors: the first captures the sunlight filtering through the entrance and reflects it towards a second, which transmits it to a third, and so on. If there were only one mirror, the cave would be less brightly lit and less extensive, and the light would soon be lost, just as the joy of being alone is lost. So it's probably hard to get a strong, lasting feeling in solitude. At best, we'll feel boredom, in other words, emptiness. And when there are already two of you, seeing a certain feeling expressed on the face of one produces an emotion in the other. Through a kind of compassion we now call "empathy", one person's feelings are communicated to the other like a mirror receives sunlight. Even in the cinema, we weep at the mere sight of a character's sadness, even

---

21. HUME (David), *Traité de la nature humaine*, liv. II, part II, section V, in *Les passions*, (trans. from English by J.-P. Cléro), GF-Flammarion, 1991, p. 213.

II. Why Say, "We Won," When we weren't Even on the Field?

though it's fictitious. Think of the tens and thousands of soccer fans who communicate their feelings to each other, making each person's emotions all the more intense.

Brains in a vat

But what do we do with all this enthusiasm and infectious energy? Not much. We exhaust it in spectacle and consumerism, even though our aspirations are "all about non-commercial things". What did we gain from the French soccer team's victory? A victory for the national team lifts the spirits of an entire country. Which, according to the statistical institutes, means more spending[22]. Personally, it's when I'm depressed that I go on a compulsive buying spree. To each his own unit of measurement. It's true that we've treated ourselves to a moment of enthusiasm. But it's not certain that we really won, or even shared anything. We weren't looking at each other like mirrors reflecting off each other. We all had our eyes turned to the screens, we didn't see each other, we didn't talk to each other. A strange form of communication. Then, if the players themselves won something, we were mere spectators. We know they're all doped, but the suspense never ceases to interest us. "Oh la la la vie en rose" is an illusion that hides people's emotional and creative misery; and "le rose

---

22. 16% more TV sets sold during the 1998 World Cup, i.e. 4.4 million instead of the usual 3.4 million. 60% of French team jersey sales are made during these major competitions.

qu'on nous propose", as the song goes, helps to divert our attention to trivial things, to keep us occupied in the same way as you keep a restless child occupied by sticking it in front of a cartoon. The rose we're offered is not a rose we can touch or smell, even if we were to prick ourselves on it. But this isn't a rose, at least we can feel something. But this is not a rose, it's the image of a rose. And this is not victory, it's an image of victory that has nothing to do with us. Even if "life in pink" has been replaced by "life in blue", it's just as illusory. It's a life by proxy.

The (tele)spectators of a match have gained all the less if they have let others act in their place. That's what *proxy voting* is all about—letting someone else put their ballot in the box. Of course, this doesn't prevent me from expressing my will, and if it's not my hand that holds the envelope, it's *my* vote that's in the ballot box. Even so, I can never be absolutely certain that the person designated voted in accordance with my opinion. It may well be a trusted person—obviously—but I'll never have an answer to the question: what happened in the polling booth? The only way to be absolutely certain that my wishes will be respected is to vote myself. So proxy voting is always about putting your fate in someone else's hands; giving up your power and always running the risk of bad consequences—in particular, the election of the candidate you didn't want. So, the proxy hardly counts as a vote. Nevertheless, the person I have appointed does represent *me,* insofar as he or she is supposed to express *my* will.

II. Why Say, "We Won," When we weren't Even on the Field?

On the other hand, what sense would there be in a sports proxy? In what sense does my team represent me? If I don't run, if I never have the ball for the good reason that I'm not even on the pitch, how can I claim to have played and won anything in this activity, this very confrontation, which I haven't experienced?

A theatre-goer watching *Romeo and Juliet* would never say "we loved each other" when the two lovers kiss, or "we're dead" when they commit suicide at the end of the play. Nor would he say "we played well" in the actors' place. Audiences can laugh or cry, since the aim is to make them feel that way. But their reactions make no difference to the drama *unfolding* before them: it's the actors who interpret it, and the story is merely a fiction already written by an author. In the theater, we know it's not real life, especially as we, as spectators, have no role to play. At best, it's a *representation* of life. When you're watching a soccer match, you're not doing sport or any other physical activity. Quite often, on the contrary, it's beer, pizza and chips on the sofa. If all it takes is twenty-two people running around a soccer pitch for twenty-two million others to shout "we've won", then we've fallen into a society of individuals who've let their lives be taken away from them. It's probably a good idea to take part in sport to maintain your body or even your mind, but most people have left it to a few to do the physical activity for them, just as they put their power in the hands of a few politicians by voting. Most people are content to watch a performance of what they would have to achieve if they were alive, but which they don't realize. Their existence would be no different if they were "brains in a vat[23]". It's as if they're watching a play, believing that the characters' lives are real and, indeed, that they're the ones on stage. This kind of identification would certainly qualify as psychiatric. And yet, you think you've played soccer, because you've seen people play soccer. Isn't that crazy?

Tomorrow morning, I won't have advanced an inch in my own life; so I'll go to work and consume, to fill the emptiness of my existence.

Alternatively, we can turn off the TV and go and play a *real* game of soccer. "Avé' les copaings".

---

23. The expression is taken from the title of the first chapter of the book *Reason, Truth and History*, written in 1981 by the American philosopher Hilary Putnam. This is more or less the idea behind the *Matrix* screenplay. If the Wachowski brothers, the film's directors, barely mention this reference, it's perhaps because the story of the "brains in a vat" quickly became a classic in the collective unconscious of American colleges. See Hilary PUTNAM, *Reason, Truth and History*, chap. I, (trans. by A. Gerschenfeld), Les éditions de Minuit, 1984.

III. Would the Result of the Match have been the Same if I Hadn't Watched It?
(Destiny and freedom)

> "If my aunt had any, we'd call him my uncle."
>
> San-Antonio

How to cork a bottle of champagne

Do you know how to re-cork a bottle of champagne? On the face of it, it's impossible, so you wonder how *they* ever got the cork in the bottle *in the first place*. At the same time, that's not really what I wanted to talk about. No, the question "Do you know how to put the cork back in a bottle of champagne?" was the joke heard after the Italians' last-gasp defeat in the Euro 2000 final. Italy were still leading 1-0 against France at the very end of the match, during the "extra time" added on to compensate for the stoppages in play, no doubt caused by an Italian who had been overdoing it.

In short, the match seemed to be over, so much so that the members of the Italian camp who had remained on the bench were already standing in onion rows, arms on each other's shoulders, ready to leap onto the pitch to celebrate their inevitable and imminent victory. For over two long minutes, they waited for the final whistle like a mere administrative formality, believing they would be European champions. And so did I.

"Well, it's dead!"

I'd already got up from my seat to change the channel and avoid watching the pointless denouement of those macaroni eaters savoring their victory.

And then… drama!

As I approached the TV to press the button, I barely saw what was happening. It was only later that I realized that Sylvain Wiltord had just scored a goal. The result: a draw at the end of normal time. And the Italians, stunned by this surprise equaliser, were soon on the receiving end of a Trezeguet goal in extra time.

So, you know how to uncork a bottle of champagne? No? Then ask an Italian!

But were the Italians wrong to uncork the champagne? Or rather, *could* they have won? Afterwards, you get the feeling that it was written—who knows where—that France had to win in the end. If I hadn't got up to turn off the TV, Wiltord would still have scored his goal. And even if I hadn't watched the match at all; if I'd preferred to go to the Festival des vieilles charrues to see the Joan

Baez concert, it wouldn't have made any difference. I imagine I would have received a call during the evening to tell me that Italy's Delvecchio had just scored a goal in the 55th minute. And later, that Sylvain Wiltord had equalised. So, once the match was over, you'd think that everything would have gone on in the same way, whatever the state of the world in general, and my own situation in particular. At the same time, you can't help imagining that changing channels can affect the course of the game: you flick on and, as luck would have it, a goal has been scored in the meantime. And I missed it! So, would the result of the match have been the same if I hadn't watched it?

Ah! If I'd seen that!

So let's assume that I didn't watch the match, as must have happened to some people trapped in an elevator or under the wheels of an old plough (if not, I don't know). The next day, someone would probably have told me about the evening: commitment, Delvecchio's goal, despair, extra time, resignation and Wiltord's goal with 10 seconds to go. And then I'd probably have said, "Ah, if I'd seen that! That's the kind of response you give to someone recounting an event you're supposed to have missed. "You missed it!" "You should have seen it!". But *could* I have even seen it? I mean, if I'd been in front of my TV, *rather* than somewhere else, would it have been the same game? When I think and say "if I'd seen it", I'm certainly imagining that

III. Would the Result of the Match have been the Same if I Hadn't Watched It?

the match would have unfolded in exactly the same way, *had I been watching it*, which at first seems obvious. Indeed, it's hard to see how the fact that I'm in front of my TV can change anything about the match. It wasn't me that Delvecchio's gang *were meeting*, despite their insistence that "we won". And we're probably a bit of idiots when we shout at the players as if they could hear us on the other side of the screen: "Look left there!" "Pass to what's-his-name!" Basically, it's not about communicating with them, it's about expressing yourself.

So whether I'm in front of the TV or not has *no impact* on the players' morale, their physical qualities and, consequently, the way the match is played. Even if I'd been in the stands, it probably wouldn't have made much difference. How could the players have heard my little voice lost in the stands?

"Shh! Listen guys! Zizou! Can you hear that? There are 52,000 fans… + one!

— Oh, that's true, Didier! I feel like I'm growing wings!"

And bang! Zidane's goal in the 60th minute. All thanks to me? Ridiculous. But what's ridiculous? When a friend tells me "You should have been there", he's probably imagining that I would have seen the match as he tells me. I'd have been just another *spectator* at this two-hour event, played out in the 55th and 93rd minutes. And yet, what would have happened if I'd been there?

First of all, at least my friend wouldn't have had the same evening: we'd have talked together, I'd have made jokes (or not) and I might even have diverted his attention when Wiltord scored. Ironically, it was my friend who missed the goal. And yet, we continue to believe that my presence had nothing to do with the match. What if my friend hadn't been there? What about his neighbor? Their whole row? The whole stand, even? In the end, it seems hard to argue that the match would have been the same if no fans had come to the stadium. Let's imagine 52,000 Italians present and no French. Would the match have gone the same way?

"Ben? Where are they? Zizou, have you seen the fans?

— Nan. I heard they went to Brittany with a cart to see John je sais pas quoi."

How many spectators do you need to turn reality or the course of the match upside down? One person doesn't count. Two probably doesn't either. What about three, four, five? Ten, twenty, fifty? One hundred, five hundred? One thousand, ten thousand? Just how many people do you think you can say: "If we'd come, things would have been very different"?

As we understand it, this is impossible to establish, because there is no precise number beyond which reality should change *more* than before. It would be like asking: how many grains of sand is a "pile" of sand? One of two things: if my presence doesn't change anything, then neither does that of the other 50,000 spectators, which is hard to believe. Moreover, it's not without the hope of somehow influencing the match that supporters of clubs or national teams are prepared to spend a lot of time and money: 238 euros for a place in the Euro 2000 final, not to mention the Thalys journey and tickets sold on the black market. But if the absence of thousands of fans is to have any consequence, then my absence *alone* can also change the course of the match. It's certainly true that if Wiltord hadn't been there, the match wouldn't have been the same. So why not me? Am I just a ghost? Even if I wasn't part of the French team on the pitch, I was still part of the world. While Wiltord was scoring a goal, I was at the Festival des vieilles charrues in Carhaix. Does this have any consequences?

The "headbutt effect" or chaos theory

On a soccer pitch, the position and movement of each player determines the course of the game. It's not for nothing that there are different tactics for arranging the ten members of a team (not counting the goalkeeper): 4-4-2, 3-5-2, 3-4-3 and so on. And if the French team ended up winning thanks to a "golden goal", it was because Trezeguet had wisely advanced close to the Italian goal when Robert Pirès crossed. However, if Trezeguet is talking to Fabien Barthez on the other side of the pitch at the same time as Pires is looking for a striker, there's no goal possible. So we can't say that Trezeguet's absence had no effect on the match, since it was he who scored. Having said that, it's also easy to see why my own situation might seem *indifferent and inconsequential.* If Trezeguet had found himself chatting to his goalkeeper, you'd have thought his presence had no impact on the match, because he was nowhere near the goal. But the fact that he was close to the goal *rather* than far away was decisive. In the same way, just because I'm in Brittany while the final is taking place in Rotterdam doesn't mean that my situation in the world has no effect on the match. After all, I could have made the trip and, like some people, run naked onto the pitch. Wouldn't that have made a difference?

The world can therefore be represented on the model of a soccer match. There is such solidarity between the players, whether team-mates or opponents, that the position and movements of each determine the actions of the others and, consequently, the course of the game. Similarly, each player's position and actions in the world must undoubtedly determine reality in one way *rather* than another. Surprising as it may seem, we have to admit that the situation at one end of the field has consequences for what happens (or doesn't happen) at the other. We come back to the idea that "the flapping of a butterfly's wings in Brazil can produce a tornado in Texas". The "butterfly effect" serves to show that there is no order in the world; that the slightest grain of sand in the clockwork of the Universe can have catastrophic consequences, or at least far-reaching effects on the system as a whole. This is what is known as chaos theory. So we can think of the world like a soccer match, as a set of elements (or players) linked together in such a way that the slightest movement of one produces effects on

III. Would the Result of the Match have been the Same if I Hadn't Watched It?

all the rest. Consequently, despite all our knowledge, such as the laws of physics, we can never predict with certainty what may happen in the future. There's always a part of things that remains *undetermined*: the flutter of a butterfly's wings, Trezeguet's movement or where I decide to spend the evening. And if we think that the world is made up of a multitude of beings and objects whose movements each produce consequences, it seems impossible to predict anything about future events. So Italy could well have won, especially if I'd been at the Rotterdam stadium rather than the Festival des vieilles charrues. Hard to believe?

First of all, it's worth remembering that a headbutt in Berlin can produce a tsunami throughout France and even the whole world. Secondly, there's no reason why the cause-and-effect relationships so visible on a soccer pitch shouldn't be found in the rest of the world. This is why certain Stoic philosophers speak of "natural solidarity" or "physics"[24] to describe the course of all events occurring in the Universe. It's the same kind of solidarity that binds the players together, whereby what happens (or doesn't happen) on one side of the field influences, causes, determines—in short, produces certain effects on the other.

If only I'd seen that! What do you mean by "that"? France's victory over Italy in the Euro 2000 final. But France beat Italy in a world where I wasn't there to see the match, where

---

24. Cicero (Marcus Tullius Cicero), *Destiny*, chap. III-IV, (trans. from Latin by Albert Yon), in *The Republic, Destiny*, Gallimard, collection Tel, 1994, p. 153.

my boyfriend was at the stadium, Joan Baez in Carhaix and David Trezeguet in front of the Italian goal. If I'd been in front of the TV, maybe my boyfriend wouldn't have seen Wiltord's goal, Joan Baez would have cancelled her concert and Trezeguet would have stayed on the sidelines. But that world doesn't exist. Was it even possible?

"A rematch?"

As you might have guessed, if we imagine that every minute of the match would have been the same, no matter what I was doing in *my little corner of the world*, it's primarily because we think that what happened was *bound to* happen. In other words, we tend to believe in Fate. "If only I'd seen that! *That, in* other words, the French team's victory, which had probably been written all along: ten seconds before Wiltord equalised, right from the start of the match, of the competition, even. Two years before, and "six hundred centuries before"[25] again. Indeed, once things have happened, we feel as if they were meant to happen, or, as the saying goes, it was written: "You missed it!" France won Euro 2000, after a match full of twists and turns. That's what happened, isn't it? So where do you get the idea that something else could have happened?

---

25. *Ibid,* chap. XII, p. 161.

III. Would the Result of the Match have been the Same if I Hadn't Watched It?

But the very idea that something else *couldn't have happened undoubtedly* stems from a kind of optical illusion. It's certain that once it's happened, France's victory can't be changed, precisely because it's in the *past.* As everyone knows, time is irreversible, so what has happened *cannot have not* happened, and that's why you can't really "remake the game". When we "remake the game" with Eugène Saccomano and Pierre Ménès, it doesn't mean we're replaying it. We simply "replay this phase of the game" and the following ones, in order to understand and explain a result that can no longer be changed. Using slow-motion replays, freeze-frames, magnifying glasses and superimposed geometrical figures, we'll show how the ball ended up in the opposing team's net. The Italians can drown their tears in the champagne they opened too early, but it won't change the result. Simply because *there's* nothing we can do about it. Does that mean we could have done something about it before, when we were still waiting for the final whistle?

The dominating argument of Diodorus and Peter Menes (but especially Diodorus)

In 2300 B.C., a certain Diodorus of Cronos, a philosopher of the so-called "Megaric" school, posed a question so sticky that it was given the name of "dominator argument". Aristotle and the Stoic philosopher Chrysippus, in particular, took great pains to try and answer it, because this argument seems to *demonstrate* that there is a Fate, and therefore that everything that happens was *bound to* happen. The French team's victory in the Euro 2000 final is not only engraved in the marble of the past; it was also carved in the crystal of the future. And if the Italians had taken the trouble to find out, they would no doubt have saved a few bottles of champagne for the 2006 World Cup, where their victory was no less certain.

This argument is very logical. It consists in showing that "any false assertion about the future expresses an impossibility." In other words, if what I predicted didn't happen, it must never have happened. Think of the sports betting offered by *Unibet*, a Scandinavian bookmaker to whom the famous Pierre Ménès sells his prognostication services to help players bet online. When you bet on a soccer result, you write the score on a betting slip, even before the match has started. Let's say I bet 2-1 for France on the eve of their final against Italy: once the match was over, I'd won because the score I'd bet on, "2-1 for France", corresponded to reality. But was my prediction right *before* the match started? In other words, *could* it have been wrong? One would tend to say yes, insofar as the match hadn't yet taken place when I filled in my ballot: Italy could have won 1-0 in the end, as we believed for so many long minutes, and I could well have lost. Yet, as we've said, once the match is over, there's also a tendency to think that nothing else *should have happened.* Is this simply a delusion linked to *the* fact that you can't change the past?

III. Would the Result of the Match have been the Same if I Hadn't Watched It?

According to Diodorus, on the contrary, it's my betting slip that proves that what happened *had to* happen and that it was simply *impossible for* anything else to happen. I wrote that France would win 2-1. However, after the final whistle, the statement "France will beat Italy 2-1 in the Euro 2000 final" became the only outcome that could be predicted. Diodorus himself could have written in the 2nd century BC: "France will beat Italy 2-1 in the Euro 2000 final". You can go back as far as you like, but the final result proves right all those who said: "France will beat Italy 2-1 in the Euro final". And the others will no doubt be said to have been wrong all along. But could those who said "Italy will beat France 1-0" have been right? Apparently not. The end of the match signals the end of predictions and the moment to reveal the right answer. The one that should have been given all along, and it doesn't matter that the event we're talking about hasn't happened yet; "any false assertion about the future expresses an impossibility." This is because a thing cannot be both possible and impossible. For example, it's impossible for a cat to grow on a tree. And it would be absurd to admit the opposite: you can't say that it's both possible and impossible for a cat to grow on a tree. It's one or the other. Now, once France have won the Euro final, it's impossible for Italy to be European champions. So, if it's impossible today, it couldn't have been possible yesterday: one thing can't be both possible and impossible at the same time. It wasn't possible for Italy to beat France 1-0, because history has shown that everyone who bet on it was wrong.

Annoying, isn't it? You can tell there's something wrong with this argument. In fact, some will think they're having trouble following it. No need to worry! It's not that you find it hard to understand, it's simply that the argument doesn't really hold water. At the same time, it's hard to find the flaw. That's what has made this sophisticated reasoning such a "dominating" argument. Aristotle and Chrysippus could see that it didn't hold water, but they had trouble explaining it. It's clear that there's a kind of sleight of hand involved here, and if Pierre Menès is good at prognosticating, Diodorus seems to have been a master of bonteau, which is a surer way of raising money. In fact, the "thing" is that two very different elements are blithely confused: on the one hand, the events that occur in reality and, on the other, what is said about them. The outcome of the match has nothing to do with my bet: "France will beat Italy 2-1". It depended entirely on the players on the pitch: Robert Pires' interception as he ran past two Italian defenders; Pires' cross and Trezeguet's interception as he got closer to the Italian goal. By a certain chain of cause and effect, things happened as they did. The question of whether the result of the match could have been different is therefore: was another chain of cause and effect possible? Could Robert Pirès have been stopped by the Italian defenders?

The lazy argument of Pierre Menès and Aristotle (but especially Aristotle)

If we can predict the outcome of a match as surely as a meteorologist can predict tomorrow's weather, it's because we assume that there are certain causes and circumstances that are bound to produce certain effects: Marcel Desailly has spent his time doing commercials, so he's not ready to play in a World Cup. What will Pierre Ménès say, for example, after predicting that France would win the Euro final on the eve of the big night? "I told you so! I was right! I'm so good at that!" In other words, the game was already decided, and the players had nothing to do with it. Indeed, if France won at the end of a chain of causes and effects predictable and foreseen by Pierre Ménès, it's because the players didn't really play. At the very least, they were merely fulfilling a destiny that had already been laid out for them.

Why can the goalkeeper who shoots the ball to make it roll predict with certainty that it will arrive at his defender's feet? Because there are laws of Nature to which objects like balls and apples are subject, and in particular, the law of inertia. When you throw a ball, it *always* rolls along the ground. Why does it do this? Because it can't do otherwise. It wouldn't be the same if the ball thought and could reflect on its actions: "Do I keep rolling or do I stop?" But we like to believe that human beings, like soccer players, are capable of thought. Why did Trezeguet score? Because he thought about it and chose to drive up towards the Italian goal, before deciding to shoot with his left foot, choosing a particular trajectory, etc. It was his choice, so much so that he was able to keep his foot on the ball. It was his choice, so no one could have predicted how he would act. However, to claim, as Pierre Ménès does, that you can predict the outcome of a match with expert certainty is to regard players as you would a physicist regard apples and balls, i.e., devoid of thought and, above all, freedom of choice. In short, when we believe that what happens was meant to happen, we assume that Destiny is fulfilled without men being able to change anything, not even the players on the pitch. But "if it's your destiny to win Euro 2000, whether you go and play or not, you'll win (…) So there's no point in going and playing.[26]" This is the "lazy" argument used by Aristotle[27] and taken up by Cicero in his treatise on *Destiny*. Clever readers will have realized that Cicero's text has been slightly altered, insofar as it doesn't mention Euro 2000, which is perfectly normal, given that soccer hadn't yet been invented in June 43, i.e. 1,957 years to the day before the Euro kicked off. That said, if there is such a thing as Fate, Cicero could well have foreseen: 1) That soccer would be invented around 1850 in England. 2) That France would win the European Cup against Italy.

---

26. CICERO (Marcus Tullius Cicero), *op. cit.*, chap. XII-XIII, p. 162-163.
27. ARISTOTLE, *De l'interprétation*, chap. IX, in *Catégories, De l'interprétation, organon I et II*, (trans. from Greek by J. Tricot), Vrin, May 3, 2000 (two months before the Euro final!).

In any case, Cicero's Fate argument is absurd. Above all, if what happened was meant to happen, the players had little to do with it, or rather, they played as it was written they would. So there's no room for freedom. Nor is there any reason to imagine that another world was possible, so it becomes pointless and false to blame the players for anything. Marcel Desailly had to let Toti's ball go through for Delvecchio to score, and then Wiltord to equalize. And in this sequence of actions, none of the players behaved in any way other than that which fate had intended. Kind of spoils the suspense, doesn't it?

IV. Can the Fans be Saved?
(Is Soccer the Nation's Last Refuge?)

"They don't push each other, they don't pile up,

Nor do they come together to make too much noise

Nor fuck to procreate until they die

Nor do they drink the blood of their so-called best
friend.

They don't run away when they're up against something stronger than they are,

Don't shit where you're not supposed to,

Don't take what doesn't belong to you.

They don't compare themselves…

Rats!"[28]

Eddie Vedder

---

28. "*They don't push, don't crowd, congregate until they're much too loud/Fuck to procreate 'til they are dead, drink the blood of their so called/Best friend/They don't scurry when something bigger comes their way/Don't shit where they're not supposed to/Don't take what's not theirs, they don't compare… rats!*", Pearl Jam, *Vs.*, "rats", Sony Music Entertainment, 1993.

If you want to know what drives the most fervent soccer fans, otherwise known as "ultras", you can listen to their songs. At the Stade Velodrome, for example, we often hear "allez l'OM… allez l'OM…". But also the less academic "*51* je t'aime, j'en boirerais des tonneaux à me rouler par terre dans tous les caniveaux". You've got to love pastis… You hear things like:

"Messins, on vous enc…"

"Parisians, fuck you…"

Of course, the "Parisians" themselves are not to be outdone. And in the catalog of their own songs, we also find the very lyrical *Marseille, Marseille on t'enc…*; a somewhat reductive title, behind which hide two rather unexpected verses:

"Marseille Marseille, on t'enc…

Marseille Marseille, on t'enc…"

So, what does that mean? No, not the insults! You can pretty much see the project. No, finding all these words on the shelf of fan classics, stadium atmosphere must-haves; what does that mean? Let's face it, soccer fans seem obsessed with sticking their willy up everyone's bum. And yet, in the sporting world, it's not uncommon to hear phrases like "we're not faggots!", which, I'm sure you'll agree, isn't very coherent. So we get a bit lost in this tangle of official declarations, and we're left to wonder: why do men who claim not to be homosexuals spend their time proposing anal coitus to other men? In short, what drives soccer fans?

Unbearable fans

One day, I saw two girls coming out of the metro behind a group of English or American girls. One of them said to the other: "You see, it's their accent that *gets on* my *nerves*". And I say to myself: why does an accent irritate her? Waiting gets on your nerves; insults get on your nerves; a screaming kid gets on your nerves. But an accent? If it bothers or annoys, it's probably because we feel disturbed or attacked by something that seems strange or foreign to us. Apparently, we tend to distrust those who are different. We're even ready to exaggerate or invent difference to give ourselves good reason to hate the other, if by misfortune he doesn't have enough strangeness: Americans speak English and, what's *more,* their accent is annoying. As far back as antiquity, the Greeks called[29] barbarians those who didn't speak their language, so that the term was synonymous with non-human. Even today, the term "barbarian" means savage, animal, devoid of humanity or civility; one who does not respect the elementary rules of life in society, such as one who gets a kick out of committing "acts of barbarism". Let's

---

29. The very term "barbarian" reflects the sounds the Greeks perceived from a foreign language they didn't understand, just as we would speak of gibberish today.

---

face it, the barbarian or subhuman is always the one who simply doesn't have the same habits as me. In fact, we think that what's wrong is simply what's wrong *with us*. Why can't we eat dog like the Chinese? If it's not like me, it's barbaric, and I tend to take my culture as the only reference for what is human. This is what Claude Lévi-Strauss calls "ethnocentrism" in *Race and History*. So, when I speak to a foreigner, I speak *louder*, as if he were deaf; as if speaking a language other than my own were a handicap. Poor thing! He doesn't understand human language and has to make do with his "foreigner", which means nothing—"couldn't speak French like everyone else!" And the ethnologist concludes: "The barbarian is first and foremost the man who believes in barbarism[30]".

Everyone's a racist or xenophobe, and so am I. We have a natural tendency to hate what's foreign to us. We have a natural tendency to hate what is foreign to us. In order to live together, we need to fight against this natural animosity: incitement to racial hatred, discriminatory practices and behavior, etc. are forbidden. Yet, in the face of these legal barriers, soccer is the perfect outlet. The world of soccer and its fans seems to be invaded by all the behaviours that perpetually threaten social unity and peace. And when we talk about supporters, the first thing that comes to mind is *hooligans* and other *ultras*, a bunch of brainless, drunken

---

30. Lévi-Strauss (Claude), *Race et histoire*, 3, Gallimard, Folio essais, 2006, p. 22.

rednecks. I don't need to remind you of all the incidents of violence in and around stadiums during matches. Deaths regularly occur at soccer matches. Racist, xenophobic or simply hateful insults are regularly hurled at referees, opposing fans, local residents or a club's foreign players[31]. Some claim that their outbursts are caused by the sporting stakes and the disappointment of seeing their team lose, all the more so when the defeat is due to a refereeing error. But the opposite may be true: sporting rivalries provide a good reason to be violent. Any excuse is good enough to get at each other[32].

Soccer philosophy? On the fan side, it seems to boil down to hatred of others. OM and PSG fans clash in the name of hatreds whose origins everyone has forgotten. On an international scale, too, xenophobic tendencies seem to be exacerbated and the clichés that fuel nationalism are reinforced, while some are trying to build a European Union: the Italians are cheats and the Germans always win without panache with the "realism" and cold efficiency characteristic

---

31. Just think of the banner displayed by Paris fans during the Lens-PSG match on March 29, 2008: "Pédophiles, chômeurs, consanguins, *bienvenue chez les ch'tis*" ("Pedophiles, unemployed, inbred, *welcome to the Ch'tis*"). In this way, the title of a film that is supposed to combat regional clichés is seized upon to reactivate them.

32. A PSG-OM match on February 29, 2010 took place at the Parc des Princes without *any* Marseille supporters. However, a PSG fan was killed… by another PSG fan. It's just that one was from the Boulogne stand and the other from the Auteuil stand.

of the Nazis[33]. Finally, there are the various friendly matches in which the North Africans whistled *La Marseillaise*. While we seek to combat racism and the tensions associated with immigration, the very people who are the victims of such tensions take pleasure in perpetuating them. We talk of the "incivilities" of these supporters, whose words and actions are contrary to the life of the city, and destroy the social body of which individuals should feel like solidary members, like the organs of a living body. In this way, fans act like a cancer eating away at the social body.

But isn't there anything for these fans to salvage?

We must save the soldier supporter

There's no doubt that fan behavior is "anti-social", even in its most hostile manifestations. On the contrary, if we look a little more closely, it's perhaps one of the most exemplary forms of solidarity. It's true that, far beyond the hooligans and other degenerates, the most fervent

---

33. You have to listen to journalists and soccer specialists. This is how Jacques Thibert, director of *France Football*, spoke of Matthaus, eternal captain of the German team, when he was awarded the 1990 Golden Ball: "After his brilliant start to the world competition (1990 World Cup), Lothar Matthäus returned to *his uniform as a soldier turned officer*, responsible for setting up *defensive markers and keeping order in the regiment*. With his *panache tucked away and his prudence slung over his shoulder*, he was [...] nothing more than the *perfect captain of a national team set on conquest and programmed to win*". *France Football*, n°2333, December 25 1990. Amazing Germanophobic expressions and prejudices!

supporters seem to be animated by feelings of animosity, particularly the *ultras*. These are the ones who light glowing smoke bombs and spread banners bearing their names, like the *Ultramarines* in Bordeaux, the *Rouge & Bleu* in Lyon or the *Red Tigers* in Lens. Yet their chants often have a warlike connotation, no doubt also expressed in their famous sodomite metaphors[34]. But the adversary that supporters designate as an enemy is no doubt only there to give the group a cause to defend, strengthening the bonds between individuals.

What is a group? And why do we want to be part of a group? It could be said that human beings don't like solitude, and that a natural feeling of friendship drives them to seek out the company of their fellow human beings. But above all, it's the best way to exist. This means first of all answering the eternal question "Who am I? What am I thinking about when I think about myself? If you do the math, most of the characteristics by which you define yourself are essentially social and given by the group to which you belong. Take the test… I define myself above all by my job, i.e. my function in society as a whole: he's

---

34. OM fans can sing: "You Messins, you're a pain in the ass, we're going to kill you all, we're going to blow you up with cocktails". On the PSG side, they sing: "In this conquest, chasing the enemy, so that our colors shine again…". In addition, the place in the stands where the ultras usually gather is called the *Kop*, in reference to a battle between the British and the Boers in the 19th century, on *Spion Kop* hill in South Africa. The sloping surface of the stands is therefore a battlefield.

a journalist, a soccer player; she's a nurse, a teacher, etc. If you don't have a job, you're not defined by it. If you don't have a job, you'll find it hard to explain what you do for a *living*, i.e. what you do, *what* you are and *who* you are. So, a woman who doesn't work and looks after her children will define herself as a mother, a housewife, while a woman who throws herself into work will define herself by this professional activity, rather than by the other elements of her life. In fact, this kind of woman is called a *working girl*, as if this were her nature and the main characteristic that defines her. And then there's my language, my nationality, my religion, my political orientation and so on. If you take all that away, it's hard to see what's left of what I think about when I think about *myself*. Even my ideas, which I might believe to be personal, come from my upbringing, from TV or from those around me. It therefore seems essential to belong to a group in order to define oneself. And in this sense, there's no evidence that being a supporter is any less essential than being a salesman or a housewife; devoting your life to a soccer team is no more ridiculous than devoting it to children who will leave one day, or to a company that may fire you after thirty years of loyal service.

All the more so since, in order to exist, we must also and above all give meaning to our lives and set ourselves goals: educating our children, earning money, saving people, and so on. To this extent, belonging to a group to serve its interests seems a good way to give meaning to one's existence:

a company seeks to sell its products or services to make a profit, a trade union seeks to defend the rights of employees, a party to conquer power and all the associations in the world give themselves a cause to defend or are based on a common interest: *Star Wars* films, creativeist philosophy or 10-meter shooting. In all cases, it's a goal that gives the group its raison d'être and its members their reasons for belonging. The advantage of soccer is that the goal is very easy to define: it's a cage made up of a 7.32-metre crossbar resting on two posts. During a match, you have to reach this goal and score as many points as possible. The season's objective is to become French champions for some teams, avoid relegation for others, or climb up to Ligue 1. And when the goal is reached, a new season begins, setting a new challenge. It's the same way with the World Cup and the Euro: as soon as you've lost, you're already looking ahead to the qualifiers for the next edition. Soccer is uncomplicated and reassuring: you know what you have to do, and the organizing bodies have a genius for dangling a carrot in front of you, notably by multiplying the number of places available for European championships between clubs[35]. Some pursue goals so obscure that it's hard to see how they

---

35. For example, the Champions League, created in 1955, was originally a competition between the league champions of each European country. Today, however, each country can send up to three or four clubs to the championship, not to mention other competitions such as the Europa League and the European Supercup. In short, just like at the fair, there are no losers: there's something for everyone!

can be achieved: to be happy, to improve society, to ensure social justice… that's all well and good, but what does it actually mean? At least when you choose to be a supporter you know you're joining a group whose goals are clearly defined and even measurable: you have to score, win points that everyone can count on. It's the kind of thing that gives life meaning, and without the headache!

So it's neither surprising nor outrageous that fans express warlike sentiments towards their opponents. First of all, any group, and especially nations, find in external enemies an opportunity to strengthen bonds. "One for all and all for one". Would this rallying cry make sense if there were no enemy or danger to confront? "All for one", but what for? There has to be another "all" against which we can unite. What could be better than a good war to rekindle the feeling of belonging to the nation that quickly takes the name of "fatherland" when it's in danger? Apparently, to feel like a "child of the fatherland", you have to find an opportunity to defend it against its enemies, as the famous *Marseillaise*, whistled by the sons of immigrants, reminds us. We want to prosecute people who are hostile to the national anthem, even though it's a song that proclaims the benefits of such behavior: if we want the members of the social body to understand that they form a single organism, we have to send them a disease against which they will have to cooperate with each other to defend themselves, and thus feel the unity that binds them. This is all the more true for soccer, which is by definition a sport of collective confrontation. But what's the point of supporting your team if you can't feel united *against* your opponent, one way or another? A soccer team only exists to meet and oppose other soccer teams. Can you imagine a team standing alone on a pitch? What for? Now, if you'd rather defend a team against *nobody*, you've only got to be a fan of 10-meter pistol shooting.

The supporter is not a spectator

Sporting confrontation is not a pretext for violence. Quite the opposite: expressions of hostility are the means —or the pretext—for strengthening the ties that bind the individuals in the group; giving each other a good reason to stand together! What common good has the wise, sofa-bound viewer served, who claims not to be a stadium enthusiast? He simply turns on the TV, curious to see if anything happens, and then runs to the rescue of victory. Indeed, we often tend to support a winning team and turn our backs on them when they lose. Whether it's a French speciality or not, the attitude of the media, soccer specialists and television viewers is as much one of rejoicing in victory as it is of shooting the ambulance. The losing team gets a bit worse off, and when they win, we find we have everything in common with them. In short, "we won", but "they lost". When you've got supporters like that, you don't need an opponent! There are people like that who joined the Resistance at the end of the 1939-1945 war.

IV. Can the Fans be Saved?

It's not very difficult to feel a sudden sense of belonging to the victorious camp, and to proclaim loud and clear that "we've won". But the question is, to what extent did you participate in the victory? Aren't most of those who shouted "vive de Gaulle" in 1945 also those who shouted "vive Pétain" in 1940? All the French may well say that their country has been liberated from Nazi occupation, but how did they themselves behave? Similarly, isn't it the fan's duty to support his team when it's doing badly, so that it can get back on its feet, rather than sticking its head under the water when it's drowning?

Fans don't just make vain incantations in front of their television sets. They've been following their team for a long time, in all places and in all situations, until they've accompanied them into the depths of the standings and even into the abyss of Ligue 2. If they are not themselves on the pitch, it's fair to say that they help the players get to the goal. They don't count the strength, time and money they spend to help their team succeed. The average fan who regularly visits his local stadium can already spend up to 60 euros per match[36]. As for the ultras, they spend a lot of time and money to buy their own equipment or to make the giant signs that adorn the stands—otherwise

------

36. In 2002, a PSG fan spent 59.50 euros per match on tickets, scarves, sandwiches and drinks. A fan of OL spends 52.20 euros, while those of OM, Le Havre, Montpellier, Lens and Bordeaux spend between 48 and 41 euros (*Le Parisien*, September 27, 2002). Look for the worst value for money…

known as *tifos*. Above all, they spend hours in the bus to follow their club's travels to the other end of the country or even abroad[37]. The fan seems to know what it's like to fight for what appears to him as a common good and a higher interest; the kind of ideal that eludes most of those who watch matches on TV and enjoy the spectacle without renouncing their individualistic tendencies. The occasional viewer lives his life vicariously in front of his television set—and "puts old bread on his balcony"—and believes he can reap the laurels of a collective adventure in which he has in no way participated. The fans, on the other hand, may well declare "we won", because they themselves are part of the forces that enabled the club to achieve victory. And given the amount of time and energy they devote to their team, it's obvious that they can identify with it, since their own existence is entirely filled by their support activities. Some go so far as to say things like: "L'OM, c'est toute ma vie" ("OM is my whole life") or "*Notre* club, celui dont les couleurs coulent dans nos veines" ("*Our club, the club whose colors* run through our veins")? Do you think that's ridiculous? I think it's ridiculous.

---

37. In the 1995-1996 season, the Bordeaux Ultramarines made twenty-five away trips. In the 2001-2002 season, they travelled to Slovakia and Sweden by minibus!

IV. Can the Fans be Saved?

Disproportionate soccer

There are some phrases that deserve to be retained by the observatory of universal bullshit standards. For example, remember the reaction to Thierry Henry's handball during the 2010 World Cup qualifier between France and Ireland: "How can France and the French still look at themselves in the mirror?" Well, wait a minute… I, for one, do just fine. Why is that? Of course, if I'd killed someone, or even if I'd cheated during a soccer game, I'd probably be ashamed. But why should I be ashamed because Thierry Henry kicked the ball with his hand? When Marc Cécillon, a former rugby international, is convicted of murdering his wife, no one but him has any idea that he *should* feel guilty. And yet, it's criminal. So, if you play rugby, you can be a *serial killer*, but if you play soccer, you're not even allowed to commit a foul, on pain of endangering the nation? Personally, I don't see what this has to do with *anything*. One might well wonder about national pride when the Prime Minister refuses to vote for the war in Iraq at the UN. And yet, despite the reaction of the United States, we can celebrate France's attitude. We can say "la France", because the Prime Minister, appointed by the President of the Republic, represents the executive power elected by a majority of the French people. So "France" here means "the will of the *majority of* the members of a nation", or at least its representatives, which is a fairly acceptable definition. But what sense does it make to identify with a soccer player?

Of course, the sporting achievements of the teams delegated by a country are important, and it's not for nothing that medals are counted so carefully at the Olympic Games. Many nations can find an opportunity to prove their worth, even their greatness, in a sporting competition. But then, is the nation itself nothing more than its soccer team? France *is* not a soccer team. At least, I don't think so. Unless a soccer match has become the only opportunity to bring life to this political body we call a nation. Because what is a nation? There are a lot of French people in France, all very different in terms of their social background, profession, religion, political orientation or foreign origin, visible or otherwise: Europeans, North Africans, Africans, Asians, etc. But if France or the "nation" is to be a nation, it has to be a nation. And yet, if France or the "nation" is indeed something, it's undoubtedly because there's at least *one* element common to all these people. And what's that? It's not just a language: French is spoken elsewhere. It's not a territory: you could very well live in a country and be a foreigner, or even *feel like one*, like all those Algerian team supporters whistling *La Marseillaise*. Conversely, there are undoubtedly nations without territory, like Palestine or Kurdistan. The nation is rather an idea shared by several individuals. It's the feeling that each one has of being a member of a whole, of a large—and sometimes sick—body. I feel French, above and beyond all the particularities that make up my life: my friends, my neighborhood, my tastes, my social milieu, etc. What do I have in common with my

IV. Can the Fans be Saved?

neighbours? What do I have in common with the other members of the nation?

Not much, apparently. We live our lives *next to each other*, without ever feeling like we*'re with* them. On public transport, in cars, on the streets or in cinema queues, we find ourselves gathered together, but deep down, the others are indifferent to us and even disturb us. Everyone seems to go about their lives without ever worrying about their fellow human beings, who are strangers to them. And the worry comes from the fact that they're there too. That's why I'd rather watch a DVD than go to the cinema, where I'd be surrounded by people talking loudly, kids bawling and phones ringing. You get the impression that you'd be freer without the presence of others. I can be attached to my family, a few friends or people who are useful to me. But apart from that, the rest of the others are just *people*, part of the scenery that bothers me more than anything else. I mean, I don't know them! I have nothing in common with them, nothing to share, except space. If you enjoyed *public transport*, you wouldn't prefer to endure more than an hour's traffic jam in your car, which you choose for the pleasure of being alone, with your own comfort and sense of freedom. If it weren't for other people, I'd be able to go out without waiting in line at the movies or exhibitions, restaurants wouldn't be full when you want to grab a bite to eat with friends; I could go on vacation without spending hours in traffic jams. They don't go to the same place as me, do they? So what are they doing here? Are they getting paid?

So it's easy to understand why Marcel Proust wrote: "There are enormous organized heaps of individuals called nations." But is the French nation anything else? For everyone to feel they belong to a group, they need to have something in common. These may be values that we believe we share with others—"liberté, égalité, fraternité" (liberty, equality, fraternity). Or it may be the pursuit of a common goal. As we've seen, *La Marseillaise* reveals that the French nation exists insofar as its members feel united in the same struggle: what unites us is that "the bloody banner of tyranny is raised against us"—except that in the song, it's said any old way, we don't know why. But what remains of this ideal of community today? Nowhere else, it seems, but in soccer.

Indeed, fans are aggressive and spend their time inventing enemies. Perhaps it's because they're trying to find a cause to fight for, to give the group a raison d'être, and thereby feel part of a collective effort. What other opportunities do we have to feel French? The national team seems to have become a refuge for the values that the French nation is supposed to embody. In this sense, there was a lot of talk about "Blacks-Blancs-Beurs" France after the 1998 victory. Why was this? Because the soccer team won a World Cup with whites, blacks and Arabs? But apart from these eleven players, does this France of successful crossbreeding exist? That's not what those famous North African fans whistling the *Marseillaise* seem to think! Apparently, there's a problem, but we're hiding it by investing what's left of the

IV. Can the Fans be Saved?

nation in a team sport. And in the end, it seems that France is nothing more than a soccer team, since it doesn't exist anywhere else.

The show business

When you've been reduced to investing all your aspirations for a common good in a soccer competition, you've found nothing else, and that's pitiful. The joy of seeing "one's" team win a match "is merely an *image* of happy unification surrounded by desolation and terror, at the quiet center of unhappiness.[38]" I'm not the one who says it, it's Guy Debord who ended up committing suicide in 1994, no doubt because he was too fed up with watching soccer on TV[39]. But it's not just the union of France's Blacks-Blancs-Beurs that's illusory. The fans who whistle the *Marseillaise* are no less pitiful! That's all they've got to express their misery and anger: booing an anthem at the start of a soccer match. The irony of history, notes Guy Debord, is "that dissatisfaction itself became a commodity as soon as economic abundance found itself able to extend its production to the processing of such a raw material.[40]" Indeed, fans who feel the fire of revolt and aspire

---

38. DEBORD (Guy), *La société du spectacle*, III, thesis 63, Folio Gallimard, 1992, p. 58.
39. However, it's hard to explain his gesture, given that OM had just been crowned European champions. Shouldn't he have been happy?
40. *Ibid*, thesis 59, p. 55.

to take part in a collective adventure are nothing more than consumers, just like everyone else. Not only does the modern world leave us all in misery, but it also uses revolt to make a little more money: we spend on gadgets, scarves, sandwiches, drinks, *tifos* and stadium passes. It's all part of a rebellion against the "system". In fact, we're sinking deeper into it. Tell me, is it the soccer results that get you so worked up?

V. "Team Spirit." Do Players only have One Brain among Them?
(What are the Values of Sport?)

"What doesn't kill me makes me stronger.[41]"

Nietzsche

"People didn't believe we were champions, even if we told them so."

You know Coluche's joke about sportsmen and women: "L'esprit d'équipe: c'est des mecs ils sont une équipe, y a *un* esprit… alors ils partagent!" But why is he so mean? Because he is! Let's face it, soccer players are better at massacring grammar than opposing teams. This is how Franck Ribéry described his debut with the French national team: "Before I went to the Stade de France, *so much so that* things went

---

41. NIETZSCHE (Friedrich), *"Was mich nicht umbringt, macht mich starker"*, *Twilight of the Idols*, in German, "Götzendämmerung", "Maximes et pointes", 8.

well for me and the training sessions, all that…" And the Boulogne accent is still missing! At the same time, that's not what we ask of sportspeople: to speak well. And it has to be said that the forgettable platitude of their speeches is not unrelated to the mediocrity of the questions put to them by journalists.

"So, Franck, big game? Do you intend to do everything to win it?

— No, no, I came to butter the sandwiches.

— Are you happy with the win, Franck? Franck, are you disappointed to have lost?"

Why spend so much time asking these stupid questions? It's astonishing that television gives hours and hours of airtime to people who have nothing to say: reactions from footballers, thoughts from starlets, even giving an hour of free expression a day to the notorious Mickaël Vendetta. Journalists and *talk-show* hosts even treat themselves to a fool's dinner with a politician, while they address Karim Benzema or Lilian Thuram with almost religious admiration. In *Sur la télévision,* Pierre Bourdieu sees the premeditated act of a *"big brother"* still distilling the opium of the people. According to him, what explains the world of TV as it is, is that "by filling this scarce time with emptiness, nothing or almost nothing, the relevant information that citizens should possess in order to exercise their democratic rights is pushed aside[42]". Without going so far as to support

---

42. Bourdieu (Pierre), *Sur la télévision,* 1, Raisons d'agir, 2008, p. 17.

a conspiracy theory, we can undoubtedly admit that this emptiness still conceals commercial interests: those of the channels, which have bought the expensive rights to broadcast the matches, and above all those of the sponsors, whose mosaic of logos always appears in the background of the interview area: we need to give the viewer time to catch a glimpse of the names of all these brands. But the footballers themselves, less idiotic than they appear, are the first to try and extricate themselves from the desert of the sports interview by attempting fine analyses instead of answering silly questions: "I think we lacked realism, etc." Alas! The players' rhetoric, designed to fill the journalists' void, itself ended up congealing into a set of ready-made expressions, soon to be echoed in the caricature of Didier Deschamps: "Well, I think it was a good match, both tequeu-nically and taqueu-tically". And the Bayonne accent is still missing!

In short, the TV that makes soccer a spectacle also produces the deplorable image that the players end up giving of themselves. But it's probably a mistake to mock sportsmen and women by declaring that there's *only one* mind for an entire team. Of course, Ribéry isn't a grammar whiz, but intelligence doesn't have a single form, and above all, it shouldn't be confused with erudition. There are people who have read a lot of books and are real morons, especially in the world of philosophy. On the other hand, you can't play soccer without being intelligent about the game. Here again, the spectacle of soccer on TV is deceptive. You get the impression that all you have to do is chase

V. "Team Spirit." Do Players only have One Brain among Them?

the ball or steal it from those who have it. And if soccer is so popular, it's probably because the rules are so simple that it's easy to understand what's going on—for all the stupid fans. Not so in rugby, a "gentlemen's" sport insofar as the complexity of the rules attracts fewer idiots: it can be hard to understand what's happening, when and why there's a scrum. But the simplicity of soccer's rules does not preclude the complexity of the tactics, which mobilize a significant amount of thought activity, invisible to the spectator. This is what professionals call the "cognitive" aspect of the sport. There are different "systems of play", and they don't all play in the same way. Everyone has seen this when a team's line-up is announced. There's the 4-2-4 (four defenders, two midfielders and four forwards), the 4-3-3, the 4-4-2, and so on. But these different combinations determine just as many ways of organizing the players' movements and the relationships between each team member. Playing soccer therefore requires reflection and, above all, solidarity. You need to know your team-mates, their physical abilities, their habits of play and movement; you need to know where they are so you can serve them better and count on their support. You have to be careful when passing the ball to an unmarked partner. Conversely, if your team's striker is too marked, you can dribble to attract opponents and allow your team-mate to be less guarded. In fact, you don't dribble to score a goal in the first place, as you always move more slowly when you have the ball at your feet. In short, the player with the ball has to look for his teammates while dribbling, and the others have to find their place in relation to the ball carrier. The player must therefore assimilate a wealth of information at the same time as making his physical effort, so much so that those who play only with their feet and lack the intelligence of the game will lose all their matches. That's how soccer is played "from head to toe".

"Know Thyself"

Soccer also demands physical qualities. First and foremost, you give yourself a good opportunity to exert yourself physically, as you would in any other sport. And that's where the fun comes from. It's easy to forget that a soccer pitch is very large (around 100 metres long), so you need strength, breath and stamina to cover the long distances to the goal. Yet, despite the image of the footballer as having a natural or divine gift for dribbling and scoring goals, we mustn't forget that he works hard. There's nothing easy about playing soccer, and the interest and pleasure we derive from it comes precisely from the effort it requires. Endurance isn't about running as fast as you can, like 100-meter sprinters. Of course, you have to be able to overtake or "outrun" your opponents to catch the ball before they do, but above all you have to keep up the pace for 90 minutes. The physical skills you need, or rather need to cultivate, are therefore quite specific and consist of a balance between speed (of running) and duration (of the match). You mustn't "burn out" in one run, nor remain too immobile on the pretext of taking it easy. In short, you need to know your own body: its power and its limits. The first reason to know your limits is to push them further, what we call "surpassing yourself". The expression doesn't actually make much sense: you can't *surpass yourself* if you want to go beyond your natural limits. It's just not possible! You only have to try to fly to understand—a little late—that you can't go beyond the limits of human nature. But it's rather "that we don't know what the body can do[43]", as Spinoza, the Dutch-Jewish philosopher of Portuguese origin, wrote—who would therefore have understood nothing of the nationalistic impulses of soccer. As a result, sport is more about going beyond what you *thought* were your limits, and discovering the power to do what you thought you were incapable of. And that's when you realize that the means may well be nothing more than the real aim of soccer: to learn to know your limits and strive to surpass them through constant effort.

For example, we talk about the warm-ups or training sessions that precede the competition, as if it were just a question of getting ready for the match, and if we run onto the pitch it's with the sole aim of scoring. But the goal is only a *means of* giving the athlete a reason to make the effort that begins in training. Indeed, sports educators

------

43. SPINOZA (Baruch), *Ethics*, part III, prop. II, scolie, (trans. from Latin by R. Caillois), Gallimard, "idées", 1954, p. 152.

believe they have noticed that if they simply time their pupils over 100 metres, they perform well below what they are capable of achieving in a soccer match. In other words, we run faster or longer when we have a goal to reach. Seeing the goalkeeper's goal at the end of the pitch, feeling marked by an opponent, trying not to lose your footing on the ball: all these attentions help you to forget that you're making a physical effort, so that you manage to overcome it. Afterwards, you'll learn that you've run kilometers for 90 minutes, or that you've clocked a 100-metre dash. In this way, you'll have discovered physical capacities never imagined before, and in the process, you'll have achieved performances beyond all previous ones, no less than the sprinter or jumper who constantly strives to beat his personal best. In other words, he's increasing his own capacity and power. Beyond victory over the opponent, then, is the footballer's victory over himself, insofar as his efforts have led him not to tire, but on the contrary, to increase his power. Joy, writes Spinoza, is "the passion by which the spirit passes to a greater perfection[44]".

The adversary is not the enemy

Soccer fans, who spend their time calling each other names and calling for bloodshed before beating the crap out of each other, haven't quite understood what they're

---

44. *Ibid.* prop. XI, scolie, p. 160.

doing here. Of course, soccer is a sport of collective confrontation, and it's victory over an opposing team that brings the joy of the famous "we've won!" But it's easy to see that the opposing team and the force they bring to bear are just another way of testing your own power. At the end of the day, even when you're up against an opponent, it's always yourself you're winning against: the opposing team is merely the resistance you face, forcing you to surpass yourself. In any case, the philosophy of confrontational sports is certainly not to regard the opponent as an enemy. This is one of the dimensions of *fair play*, which often obliges players to shake hands at the end of a match, whatever the result. It's not primarily a question of playing by the rules, but of nurturing a feeling of solidarity, even friendship, towards one's opponent. You should see tennis players at the end of a match. They don't look at all like two enemies. They share the same goal, and they know they can only achieve it by playing against each other. In fact, you get the feeling that the longer a tennis match lasts, testing the physical and mental endurance of the players, the closer they feel to each other. Above all, this is because they understand each other's pain insofar as they feel the same; and they probably know that no one else can understand what they've just endured. There is nothing in this compassion, this solidarity in suffering, this very friendship, that resembles the feelings we have towards an enemy. "Enemy" comes from the Latin *inimicitia*, enmity, the opposite of friendship, and in fact, hatred. And as we all know, we tend to feel this way about people we know little or not at all, and who we refuse to get to know. This is what we see in all forms of racism and xenophobia: the simple fear of what is different and what we don't understand, a language, a skin color or customs different from our own that we reject because we find nothing familiar in them. But you can't win against a foreign opponent. On the contrary, you have to get to know him well; know what his strengths are so you can work on resisting them—his serve, the speed with which he moves—and what his weaknesses are so you can exploit them—his backhand, his groundstrokes. This task is all the more complex in soccer, where you need to know the whole team. You need to know the abilities of each member of the team—which one to watch out for, how, how much? You also need to know the different systems that opposing players use to play with each other: defensive, offensive; forward or backward? In short, you have to play according to the way the opposing team plays. You have to know your enemy, which means not making an enemy of him.

Force is not violence

When you stick a bicycle wheel on a tennis player—an old 6-0/6-0—you hardly look at him. Sure, we won the match, but we were a little bored. That's because we didn't find what we'd come for: the feeling of his power. In sport, the joy of victory is felt all the more when you've

V. "Team Spirit." Do Players only have One Brain among Them?

beaten strong opponents, even superior to yourself. It's the only way to feel an increase in power. As the saying goes, "To conquer without peril is to triumph without glory". But it's rather that without peril, you triumph without joy, and in fact, you don't triumph at all, since you've defeated forces you already knew to be inferior to your own. Only the weak attack those smaller than themselves to give themselves the illusion of being strong. Here again, the sporting adversary is not an enemy. When you go to war, you probably prefer a weak enemy to avoid damage. This is because war is only a means to an end, and we have other ends in mind: conquering territory or eliminating populations towards whom we feel hatred, for all the bad reasons that Nazis, fascists, racists and xenophobes do. "Attack is in my instincts", wrote Nietzsche, who has often been caricatured as a kind of Nazi. But read on: "The task is *not at all* to master resistance of all kinds, but to master resistance against which one must commit all one's strength, flexibility and mastery of weapons—*equal* opponents… To confront the enemy on equal terms—the first condition of a *fair* duel. When you despise, it's *impossible to* make war; when you have the upper hand, when you see things *from above*, you *don't have* to make war.[45]"

---

45. Nietzsche (Friedrich), *Ecce homo*, "Why I am so wise", 7, (translated from the German by Éric Blondel), GF-Flammarion, 1992, p. 66.

And what puts us on an equal footing is, first and foremost, obedience to the same rules. Some people think it's impossible to play well and win against a beginner who knows nothing about the game. It's a bit of an excuse, but it's also true. It's important to follow the rules, because you learn to respect others and yourself. What is respect? It's a very difficult word to define. It's used in all sorts of ways, especially by those who have no respect for anything or anyone. A suburban *kaira* will happily say, "Hey, you disrespected me!" And this kind of individual confuses respect with submission imposed by violence. He thinks he's respected when others are afraid of him. He's completely mistaken. We say "respect silence", or "respect the dead", authority and others. What does this mean? In all cases, there's the idea that we feel obliged to what we respect. We forbid ourselves to behave in certain ways. Respect comes not from others, but from ourselves. It's a feeling that's hard to define, and one that demands restraint. We know that we can't and shouldn't act in any way, because we attribute a certain value to what we respect. Respect means accepting to limit oneself to make room for silence, for the dead, for others. To respect your opponent is to feel that you have obligations towards him, not all the rights. Sporting confrontation has nothing to do with the law of the strongest, if by that we mean the law of the most violent. Another way of avoiding Nietzsche's misunderstandings of the strong and the weak. In a tennis match, the strongest player is the one who wins according to the rules: who beats his opponent evenly, because that's the best way to show his superiority. This means he uses all the qualities required: intelligence—of the game—endurance, courage, self-control and the technique he has learned. On the other hand, when a player starts to lose, he sometimes gets angry, throws his racket on the ground, shouts, insults the referee or lashes out at the audience. But when you throw your racket in your opponent's face, you're not stronger at all. You're weaker, and that's why you become violent. You haven't been able to prove your power: impatient, a poor technician, unable to run to catch balls. So, strength is measured first and foremost by obedience to the rules, and victory can only be savored if the rules are obeyed. You're strong first and foremost because you've been able to channel and direct the physical power within you: not by throwing your racket at the other player, but by delivering an *ace* at 200 km/hour. You're also strong because you've beaten the other player on equal terms, which means you owe your victory solely to your own efforts and not to any initial inequality.

Camus is not Canio

It's almost easy to understand the words of Albert Camus, winner of the Nobel Prize for Literature in 1957: "Everything I know for *sure* about the morality and obligations of men, I owe to soccer." Soccer as a school of self-respect and respect for others. Camus was a goalkeeper with Racing Université d'Alger, long before he became a philosopher and writer. He would almost have become a professional footballer if the first pains of tuberculosis had not put an end to his ambitions, around 1930. But this footballer figure cuts through all the jokes about sportsmen and women, such as: "He's not a Nobel Prize winner!" Because *he is* a Nobel Prize winner!

At the same time, it's hard not to think of Paolo Di Canio, the Lazio striker who spent most of his career in Italy (1985-1996) and England (1997-2004). He is widely recognized as having the talent and technique of a great player. His dribbling skills enable him to evade half a dozen defenders before scoring a goal in the process, with the instep of his foot. Above all, he was awarded the FIFA *Fair Play* award in 2001, after distinguishing himself in an English championship match between his West Ham team and Everton. With the opposing goalkeeper down and injured, one of Di Canio's team-mates took the opportunity to cross for him. But instead of scoring the goal, the Italian player grabbed the ball with his hands to suspend play. It was beautiful! Paradoxically, he received a thirteen-match suspension for assaulting a referee during a match against Arsenal in 1998. Not to mention the fascist salute he gave his fans at several matches. What class! It's hard to see soccer as a school of morality: despite *a fair-play* gesture, there's no respect for refereeing and therefore for the rules. Violence rather than strength. As for the fascist

V. "Team Spirit." Do Players only have One Brain among Them?

salute, it shows the player's nationalist sentiments and worship of the law of the strongest, contrary to everything we've tried to show. Clearly, Paolo Di Canio has the same spirit as those fans who would like to stick their willy up everyone's bum—"you're fuckers, we're going to kill you". Like them, Paolo Di Canio doesn't have opponents, he has enemies.

We're sure you'll agree that this is just one example. But it's only an *extreme* case. However, if we take a closer look, we'll see that most professional footballers behave in a way that is totally contrary to the spirit and values of the sport. No respect for the rules and cheating whenever they can. Thierry Henry's hand, for example, is on a par with that of Maradona, another soccer god. But it's all the players who seem to spend their time disputing the referee's decisions or demanding compensation. As soon as two opponents fight over the ball and kick it out, they raise their hands to the sky to tell the referee that "it's not me, it's the other guy". They always exaggerate their pain and the movement of their fall when an opponent has fouled their fragile little body—not to mention those who dive without being pushed. This is how athletes who are supposed to be testing their will to power end up dropping like flies as soon as someone brushes up against them. "Hello Mommy Boo!" Is this the Nietzschean superman? We're also a little surprised when players and fans seem relieved when the draw is "favorable". If it's your own strength that you're testing, you should be delighted to find yourself in the so-called "group of death". And we much prefer a team that is happy to meet a scarecrow: Brazil in soccer, New Zealand in rugby. And then there's doping, which not only involves cheating, but also empties sport of all those ideas of mastering one's body and surpassing one's limits. That's how we see 20-year-olds end up dead in the middle of a match from cardiac arrest—like Marc-Vivien Foé or Puerta.

As for money, it's a real nuisance; another way of cheating by putting together so-called "dream teams" with millions of euros, like Real Madrid. First of all, it's contrary to the ideal of equality between opponents. We're trying to create a kind of over-team like no other. And in any case, you lose all the team spirit and solidarity that seemed to count for so much. This kind of club is not a team, but an accumulation of individual players who know no one but themselves. And money turns pseudo-supermen into by-products. Proud commodities costing millions of euros. This is how poor Christiano Ronaldo, winner of the 2008 Ballon d'Or, came to be known as "the most expensive man in the world"[46]. Players are bought, lent and sold like luxury slaves. There's even a name for it: *mercato*, which simply means "market" in Italian. Consumer society is so fond of the term that it is now used for television, so much so that it can be taken

---

46. Transferred to Real Madrid for the 2009-2010 season for 94 million euros.

to mean human trafficking. And that's what all little children would like to become: slaves[47].

____

47. The final bloody act of this comedy is represented by *Football Cracks*, a kind of soccer "American Idol", sponsored by Zidane himself, who seems to have lost his way a little. Contestants not only have to know how to play soccer, they also have to speak in front of a camera. It's easy to see that soccer stars aren't role models at all because they play soccer, but because they're stars. If little children want to "become Zidane", it's not in the sense that they want to become great soccer players. It's not even in the sense that they want to become the greatest soccer player of all time. "Becoming Zidane" simply means becoming a "star", a *celebrity*, with all the clichés of happiness that seem to go with it, and above all, the ideal of an "easy" life and money, absolutely contrary to everything that makes up the spirit of the sport.

VI. Does the Referee get Paid?
(What is Justice?)

> "Is the referee getting paid or what?
> — Of course he gets paid! He doesn't work
> for free, either!"
>
> *Didier*

Death to the referee!

What would become of post-match shows if we had nothing to say about refereeing? We're used to denouncing referee errors that seem to spoil the pleasure of a match or the taste of a victory. But do we really want them to go away? Refereeing errors are part of the game. Not in the sense that we can't prevent them from happening, but in the sense that they contribute to the spectacle of soccer and the pleasure we take in watching it, in the same way as goals scored or the more or less remarkable talent of the players. Why do we refuse to help referees with video, if not to safeguard "refereeing errors"? They undoubtedly allow fans to add a sensitive string to their bow: hating the referee too, and thereby finding an additional bond to strengthen the group. They also allow commentators to comment. Refereeing errors are just as much a part of match analysis as combinations or penalties. Last but not least, it's a chance for occasional viewers to "rewatch the game" over a beer.

But if you want to replay the game, you have to have something to criticize. We can't just talk about the best actions and goals, like recalling the best lines from a film we loved.

"Did you know Carole dumped me?

— Oh no… Does that mean you're on your own now?

— Oh yes, Sherlock Holmes! Since it was just the two of us… It wasn't a cult!"

Of course, repeating the lines from a film like *Delphine 1 Yvan 0* is absolutely pointless, since everyone repeating them has heard them before. And yet, it's probably enough to provoke another round of laughter, which is the very essence of enjoyment of this kind of film. But when it comes to soccer, it's hard to recapture the excitement of a match simply by talking about it. At best, the images can be replayed. But how well can you "replay the game" with your friends? If there's nothing to talk about other than one team's victory over the other and its indisputable superiority, you'll soon get bored. And since we can't always find a generous Zidane willing to take a swipe at the ball to start a discussion, we have to find a way to keep the popular fervor going. Fortunately, there's the referee!

Refereeing errors can be discussed for hours after matches. And at the same time, the debate about refereeing reform. But if we really reformed this part of the game, as some people *claim to* want, we'd perhaps have nothing more to talk about. And I, no less than anyone else. With refereeing errors, the viewer will have something to talk about, the "specialist" something to debate and the fan something to hate. In short, everyone convinces themselves that it's the beauty of the game that appeals to them, or even the honor of victory; even chauvinism would be a laudable motivation. But deep down, it's possible that what we like in all this is the *nastiness.* The inconsequential nastiness that soccer allows us to maintain or unload, and for the satisfaction of which we offer referees as fodder for (tele) spectators. And the coaches too.

Man is a viper's tongue to man

Let's reminisce about the schoolyard. What are teenagers' favorite topics of conversation? Talking badly about others, of course! And when you've run out of people to talk to, you get bored. We lie to ourselves, pretending that we wouldn't want to surround ourselves with hateful people; that we'd rather not waste time worrying about those we hate. But when it comes down to it, we enjoy talking about the foolishness of those we hate far more than the good deeds of those we claim to love. This is how Thomas Hobbes, the seventeenth-century British philosopher, remarked "how

VI. Does the Referee get Paid?

everyone delights above all in things that make people laugh". It's not friendship for others that drives us to get together, it's that with them, "we prick up the absent, we examine their whole lives, all their actions are put on the carpet, we make them subjects of mockery, we peel back their words, we judge them, and we condemn them with great freedom. [...] These are the real delights of society[48]". This may sound like a very cynical view of human nature and society. But what if it were true? Hobbes does not believe that men are capable of feeling the slightest sympathy for their fellow men. It's selfishness, self-interest and personal pleasure that drive everyone to act, even when seeking companionship. We would therefore have no gregarious instinct and no pleasure in living in a group. According to Hobbes, man is a solitary animal with no good feelings towards others, and even the most seemingly generous actions are explained by selfish intentions. Indeed, why do we perform "good deeds" if not to boost our self-esteem and satisfy our pride? When we help the old lady cross the road, or donate money to the good causes sponsored by a Zidane, it's undoubtedly to hear ourselves say: "I really am a good person!" And the sports star himself must no doubt be looking for the same thing when he puts his celebrity at the service of a good cause. Isn't it rather the good cause that serves his celebrity?

---

48. HOBBES (Thomas), *The Citizen*, "Liberty", chap. II, (trans. from Latin by S. Sorbière), GF-Flammarion, Paris, 1982, p. 91.

One day, I was on the shuttle bus to the Fête de l'Huma, where the values of liberty, equality and fraternity are supposed to be celebrated. On the bus, next to me, two high-school girls spent the entire journey bad-mouthing a girl they knew. After half an hour, one of them, no doubt struck by a flash of lucidity, asks the other: "Say, I hope you don't talk about me like that when I'm not around!" This, Hobbes concludes, "makes me greatly approve the advice of the man who always withdrew last from a company." And me!

Ravanelli

Fabrizio Ravanelli. For those who are unfamiliar with this Italian player from the 1990s, or have forgotten him, it was his time with Olympique de Marseille that gave him his claim to fame. Fabrizio Ravanelli is the biggest simulator in the history of the French Championship, if not the whole world. And it was on the evening of November 9, 1997, that he reached the pinnacle of his career, during the PSG-OM "classico" played at the Parc des Princes. With the score tied, Ravanelli raced towards the opposition goal. When he entered the penalty area, Paris defender Éric Rabesandratana was still breathing down his neck. A little too much perhaps, as he appears to trip Ravanelli, who dives to the ground. The referee whistled for the penalty, and Ravanelli's team-mate Laurent Blanc took it. A goal and a 1-2 victory for OM. The problem is that in slow motion, it's hard to see the defender's foul. What is clearly visible, however, is Ravanelli tripping over himself, bringing his right leg behind his left, before diving into the net. That day, the Marseille fans probably didn't insult the referee too much…

It's fair to say that OM's victory was completely undeserved. The referee made an obvious mistake by whistling for a foul that didn't happen. It's just as unfair as France's victory over Ireland in the World Cup qualifiers, when the referee failed to see Thierry Henry's foul. It's unfair because the players aren't punished in accordance with the rules of soccer, what in more official terms are known as the "Laws of the Game". So, we can always argue about an offside that even the video has trouble confirming. But Ravanelli and Thierry Henry committed what the refereeing authorities call "gross fouls". They demonstrate unsportsmanlike behavior. They must therefore not only be punished by a free kick awarded to the opposing team like all "normal" fouls, but the player must also be shown a yellow or red card. However, there's a crude foul with a very familiar name when you consult the *Laws of the Game, namely* "simulation": "A player attempting to deceive the referee by feigning injury or pretending to be the victim of a foul is guilty of simulation." Instead of "player", we could probably have written "Italian" and, just as we speak of "Fosbury" in the high jump, to designate the figure of the same name, we could have christened "Ravanelli", the foul committed by the player of the same name.

So we're quite right to be up in arms about these "gross" refereeing errors, and it's certainly not for the pleasure of bad-mouthing the referee that the PSG *staff* and players have taken it out on him. There is simply the honest, deep and painful feeling of having been "screwed". Who could claim that the referee's error was not a regrettable accident, and one that was badly experienced by those who suffered the injustice of his decision? No one could. But isn't it rather that we tend to find any decision unfavourable to our own team unjust—as if by chance?

Fault for some, *play fact* for others

It's funny how we're more likely to see our opponents' fouls than those of our own team. And even what appears to be a foul to some is merely a fact of play to others. In fact, "play fact" is an expression that has been part of soccer vocabulary for some time now, and has two meanings: 1) A foul that the referee has not seen. 2) A foul committed by my team that I refuse to consider a foul. Thus, in reference to Thierry Henry's handball, Laurent Blanc was able to say:

"It's a fact of play that was in our favor, like others in the past."

Of course! You can't say "it's a foul that was in our favor", otherwise you're going to get your head handed to you by FIFA. In this way, the philosophy of soccer seems very close to that of Hobbes, according to whom "each one names

VI. Does the Referee get Paid?

well what he would like to have done to him and *badly* what he would like to avoid[49]", in other words, what some people call *a game fact*, others call a *foul*. It all depends on which team you're on. For example, it's not certain that the famous Laurent Blanc has fully digested Bilic's simulation during the 1998 World Cup semi-final. You may recall that the French player slapped the Croatian in the face, before the latter fell to the ground writhing in pain, his hand glued to his eye, even though it wasn't where he'd been hit. A red card and Laurent Blanc's expulsion, depriving him of the final against Brazil. However, it was the same Laurent Blanc who had taken the penalty for Ravanelli's simulation, without asking too many questions. So it's easy to imagine how the same play can appear to the same player as a foul or not, depending on whether it benefits him or not.

Thus, the notions of justice and injustice seem eminently relative, and Hobbes seems to be right when he states that we call "just" that which is beneficial to us and unjust that which is harmful to us. Players, fans and television viewers are always inclined to consider a foul committed by their team as negligible. At the end of the day, the most important thing is to get close to your opponent's goal. We'll always be very observant when it comes to opponents' fouls that earn a free kick, and much more indulgent towards our own team's "facts of play". "But no! It's not a foul! Stop rolling on the floor!" When a player on my team rolls on the floor, it's

---

49. Hobbes (Thomas), *op. cit.* in "The Empire", chap. XVII, p. 252.

because he's hurt, and if it's an opposing player, he's faking. Consequently, if we want to ensure peace in society in general, and a little order in soccer in particular, "we must not judge what is reasonably to blame, by the reason of one, rather than by that of the other[50]". There can be no doubt that everyone thinks they are right. And even Ravanelli says to this day that Rabesandratana was responsible for his downfall. Is he lying? Perhaps not. He probably *believes* what he's saying. Because when it comes down to it, what motivates people's judgments is not justice, but their own advantage, so that they tend to interpret all the facts of the game through the prism of their own particular interests. It's only human, and players are the first to know it.

That's why they probably prefer to rely on the decision of a third party, i.e. the arbitrator.

What indeed is an arbitrator? An arbitrator is someone appointed to settle a dispute between two parties, like a judge in a court case. If we simply waited for the two parties to come to an agreement, we could wait a long time, for the good reason that *they are opposed to each other.*

Man is a wolf to man

If you look at the way players behave even when there's a referee, you can imagine what it would be like if there wasn't one, and just how essential his presence is. Just think

---

50. *Ibid*, p. 253.

VI. Does the Referee get Paid?

of what happens when two players fight over a ball that ends up going over the goal line: everyone throws up their hands and gestures to the referee to explain that it was the other player who took the ball out. For one, it's a *corner*, for the other, it's a *goal clearance*. Soccer players always look like irresponsible kids who defer totally to the referee, and it would be hard to see any *fair play* in their behavior, i.e. a way of "playing with a spirit of justice". What is justice? It means giving everyone what they deserve. It's hard to find justice in the way the various teams on the pitch interpret the game. No matter how honest they may be, a team's players, *staff* or fans will always tend to see things in terms of the pleasure they derive from them, or not. Basically, the opposing parties in a soccer match never seek to receive what they deserve according to the laws of the game, but only what they want. Certainly, if I like a team and support it, I immediately consider that it deserves to win. So it's neither the players nor the fans who should be asked for their opinion on the justice of a decision. "You can't be both judge and jury.

If there were no referee, if the players assessed their own faults and penalties, we'd probably never get to play, and worse, the match would soon end in a pitched battle, as it sometimes does, even though there is a referee. In the dedication that precedes *The Citizen*, Hobbes recalls the formula: "Man is a wolf to man". It's not really that man is "evil", it's just that he's selfish: everyone's only concern is to serve their own personal interests, and the interests of some often conflict with those of others. In soccer, this is obvious, as there is only one ball for two teams, and each team tries to get close to the other's goal. In short, a confrontational sport such as soccer offers an exemplary model of a situation where the interests of some are strictly opposed to the interests of others. As a result, it's "everyone against everyone". But as long as there are no rules, or as long as it's up to each party to judge what's fair and what isn't, the war drags on and on, and above all, there is no justice, since each party considers as fair what's in its own interest.

On the contrary, the referee is supposed to have no interests that bind him to one side rather than the other. For example, the referee in the match between France and Ireland had to be of a third nationality, in this case Swedish. Furthermore, it is assumed that he was not "paid" by either team to favor it, otherwise he would have had an interest. Of course, the referee's decision is based on rules we all know: in soccer, he is supposed to enforce the laws of the game, just as a court judge relies on the law. Nevertheless, his decision is sovereign and must be considered as such. This means that the referee has the last word, so his decision, whatever it may be, cannot be discussed. It is for this reason, moreover, that one is not allowed to comment on a court decision. This is essential, because the referee is appointed precisely to put an end to disagreements: to distinguish between what each party claims in its own interest, in order to give each party what it deserves, in the interests of the game.

There's no such thing as a refereeing error

In English, the *referee is* called a *referee, which* means that he or she is considered by everyone to be *the* authority on the rules. Basically, that's what everyone wants. If we have to refer to a player from one of the two teams, no matter how *fair-play* he may be like Laurent Blanc, we can suspect that he will call few fouls against his team. Nobody would want one of the players as a referee. So, what do we do? We ask someone with nothing to lose or gain from the match to decide whether the rules of the game are being followed, *for all the actions of all the players.*

It's true that the referee's decisions are always debatable, because they concern facts that are difficult to establish. For example, to what extent is a hand a hand, intentionally or not? Is it an elbow rather than a hand? Did the defender touch Ravanelli or not? So many heads, so many opinions, and to tell the truth, the alleged simulation by the former OM player is still being debated today. But that's precisely why we need to at least agree on a referee who will decide for everyone. He's a man, he may make mistakes, he may have certain preferences—who knows? But we decide to consider his personal interpretation as the only truth, especially as it is at least guaranteed by his neutrality. And that's what we call respect for the referee's decisions.

So, in formal terms, the referee's decisions are in fact indisputable. We can indeed speak of a "refereeing error" if we consider that the referee's decision does not comply with the rules. But the problem is that the referee is *the only person* authorized to judge the correct application of the rules. It is therefore impossible to talk about refereeing errors, since the very nature of refereeing is to have the last word. Ultimately, only the referee can accuse himself of a refereeing error. And if the referee's decisions are challenged, a new referee will have to be found to arbitrate between the referee and those who challenge his decision. As we understand it, someone has to decide in the end, anyway. Did the referee make a mistake? Who says so? The PSG players? But right from the start, we recognized that we couldn't rely on the footballers' opinion, because their decisions would always be more unfair than those of a referee. Allowing everyone to question the referee's decisions would be like allowing everyone to disobey the law when they don't like it. The referee is always right, not because he is right, but because he is the referee. And once you've appointed him, you've given up discussing his decisions, whatever they may be, just like Laurent Blanc, who never denounced any refereeing error, even when it went against him.

If we're not happy, all we have to do is change soccer's refereeing rules, and admit the use of video. But what can we talk about afterwards? And who are we going to be able to speak ill of? In the end, we're quite happy to be able to replay the match through these refereeing errors, which are not for nothing in the success of soccer.

VII. Why are Women Incapable of Understanding *Offside*?
(Does being Free mean Obeying no Rules?)

> "A being feels obliged only if it is free."
>
> Henri Bergson

What is offside?

Why don't women understand the offside rule? The first obvious answer is: because they have trouble *understanding* things in general. On average, their brains are smaller than men's, and according to scientists, women are more gifted with interpersonal skills than intellectual ones. And then, when my wife passes in front of the TV screen to bring me a beer, firstly, she bothers me, and secondly, she doesn't have time to take it all in. She can see that a bunch of guys in shorts are fighting over a ball, and that they're *roughly heading* for the sieve-shaped gantry at the end of the pitch we call a goal. As she passes by a second time to clear the table, she can deduce that a player is throwing the ball back "into touch" because it has gone out of bounds. That way, until it's time to put the kids to bed, she can keep an eye on the game for a while longer, and see what distinguishes a *corner* from a goal. The problem is, with so much to do at the same time, and so little time in front of the TV, she won't be able to understand the most important rule of soccer, the one that gives the sport its nobility: offside.

TV. — *Offside!*
Bobonne. — What's all this about offside?
Me. — You wouldn't understand, it's a guy thing, male perfection *(I burp.)*… Can you get me a beer?

That said, even if a woman tries to follow soccer more assiduously, she'll still have trouble integrating the offside rule because of her simplistic deductive mind. Indeed, it appears that a woman has great difficulty switching off a computer because she first has to click on the "start" tab in the left-hand corner of the screen. Gifted with rudimentary logic, she thinks that "start" is for starting. In the same way, you'd first have to explain to her that "offside" doesn't mean that a player isn't playing. He's not out of the game or excluded: he's still on the pitch. "Offside" does not mean "on the sidelines" or "on the sidelines" or out of bounds. I say this just in case; I'm trying to put myself in their shoes and understand why they don't understand. Nonetheless, they'll agree that while the footballer is not excluded, he is, in *a certain sense,* banned from the game.

From Head to Toe

To put it simply, he's not allowed to take part in the game, to touch the ball, as long as he's in the famous "offside" position. Why is this? It's hard to say. It's something a man understands intuitively. Offside is a particular position occupied by a player, defined as follows: if a player is placed on the pitch in such a way *that there are not at least two players (including the goalkeeper) between him and the opposing goal.*

Note that the rule only applies to players who don't *yet have* the ball. In fact, if cute Nuno Gomes is running with the ball towards the goal, he has every right to arrive alone in front of the keeper. A goal has to be scored eventually. So offside never concerns a player *carrying* the ball, but only a player *not carrying it.* Imagine, for example, a match between Italy and Portugal. Sexy Nuno Gomes, the ball carrier, dribbles towards the opponent's goal. There, the handsome Cristiano Ronaldo, not carrying the ball, waits for his team-mate near the goal of Buffon, the torrid Italian goalkeeper. Ronaldo is offside if he's alone against Buffon. In this case, there is only one player between the striker and the opposing goal—the goalkeeper. On the other hand, if the dashing Italian defender Cannavaro is between Ronaldo and Buffon, the Portuguese striker is not offside, since there are two players between him and the opposing goal, namely Buffon and Cannavaro: 1 + 1 = 2 (you're allowed to reread if that's too difficult for you).

If Christiano Ronaldo is offside and alone in front of the goalkeeper, he has no right to take part in the game.

VII. Why are Women Incapable of Understanding Offside?

This means that Nuno Gomes, who is approaching, cannot throw the ball to him, and if he does, a linesman will blow his whistle to indicate that Ronaldo is "offside". As a result, if the Portuguese striker ends up scoring a goal, it won't be counted, since he wasn't supposed to catch the ball; he had no right to take part in the game given his position on the pitch. On the other hand, if Cannavaro is there to help Buffon defend the Italian goal, Nuno Gomes can pass to Christiano Ronaldo and give him the chance to score. So, ladies, you might be lucky enough to see the handsome Portuguese stripping off to celebrate his goal.

The slow agony of offside

In fact, if women don't understand the offside rule, it may be because they don't want to, given that soccer is an essentially male sport. In fact, according to official figures, the sport has the fewest women, less than rugby and motor-cycling[51]. Are they therefore put off by the complexity of the rules? This is doubtful, given that soccer is the *world's simplest* team sport, with just two rules:

1) The object of the game is to get a leather ball into the opponent's goal, using any part of the body *except the hands* and arms.

---

51. 3% of licenses issued to women in soccer, 3.8% in rugby and 5.1% in motorcycling (Insee, 2007).

2) A player is *offside* (and therefore cannot apply rule no. 1) if there are not two players between him and the opponent's goal.

You guys all right? Not too difficult to assimilate these *two* rules of the game? Apparently so. Professional players, the ones who are paid to play the game from morning to night and *vaguely* remember the rules, have a hard time doing it themselves. For a start, even a great player like Thierry Henry, even a soccer god like Maradona[52], has trouble understanding rule no. 1, which means they don't really know what soccer is all about. Indeed, rule no.1 simply defines soccer as *foot-ball,* *i.*e. a ball game played with the foot. But most men seem to have just as much trouble understanding *offside* rule no.2, insofar as many would prefer it to disappear (which would reduce soccer to *a single rule,* incidentally). To read and hear the comments of a certain number of people, starting with soccer players, *offside would disturb* the progress of a match; it would be an embarrassment, an obstacle even to the game. First of all, the rule seems a little absurd. Either you play or you don't play. But it's strange to declare a player "offside" when he's

---

52. Diego Maradona scored a goal with his hand against England in the 1986 World Cup, which enabled Argentina to open the scoring and qualify for the semi-final before going on to win the World Cup. This goal has since been attributed to "the hand of God". Need we remind you that Thierry Henry, for his part, made a decisive pass with his hand to help France qualify for the 2010 World Cup finals against Ireland? But as Thierry Henry is no Maradona, he was awarded the "hand of shame" instead.

on the pitch and capable of scoring a goal. Isn't that unfair? You've played the ball, scored a goal and now you're told you're "offside". What's more, this rule is often the pretext for yet more disputes and disputes about refereeing, which we could do without. You can see this from the slow-motion replays on TV, which often give rise to controversy over whether or not a player was offside. Above all, the offside rule seems to slow down the pace of a match. If it weren't for the offside rule, the attacking player in a hurry would be able to score his "dose" of goals without having to wait for all the other players on the pitch to join him! Understandably, this would allow a lot more goals to be scored in soccer, which would add a bit of action and perhaps make the game less boring[53].

I do as I please

Would the attacker really be freer if there were no offside rule? In fact, this assumption is based on the idea that to be free is to obey no rules. What is freedom? How free do we feel? At first glance, it's when you do *what you want*. I feel that in the morning, I'd be freer if I didn't have to drag

---

53. Soccer's governing bodies themselves have made successive changes to the rule, seemingly with the aim of reducing or even erasing its influence on the match and giving more *freedom* to the forwards. Originally, a striker was offside if there were not *three* players between him and the goal, and in 1925 the number was reduced to two players. Since 1990, it has been sufficient for the striker to be on the *same line* as the last defender.

myself out of bed because of the alarm clock ringing, and it's not without a certain pleasure that we look forward to those "late mornings" at the weekend. To be free is to *feel* free, which means nothing more than doing things with a sense of *ease*. Acting spontaneously. How else to put it? Staying in bed is *effortless, which is not the* case when you have to get up. So as soon as you have to make an effort, you're not free, which manifests itself in a feeling of obligation: I feel "obliged" to get up. This means that if it were up to *me*, I'd stay in bed. "If it were up to me!" This expression helps us understand both what freedom is and where the feeling of not being free comes from. If it were up to me, if I were all alone in the world, I'd have no obligations to get in the way of what I want to do. I'd stay in bed, I wouldn't go to work, I'd drive at 200 km/h and score a goal without worrying about my position on the pitch. In this sense, I'm not free insofar as I have to do what someone or something other than myself wants me to do: what someone asks or commands me to do, such as my boss, my parents, the referee and, in general, other people.

On the contrary, freedom consists in simply following the course of one's desires and desires as they arise. Basically, to be free is to do as I please. Of course, I'm not sure why I want to stay in bed, but I do know that I'd feel much less free if I forced myself to get up. So, we imagine that we'd be freer if there were no rules, starting with legal laws. If it were up to me, I wouldn't pay my taxes, my bills or my parking, and I'd even park anywhere. In the same way, a soccer player must feel that the rules of the game and *offside are an* obstacle to his freedom. All he cares about is scoring, and if it were up to him, he'd go straight for the goal and try to shoot. But the offside rule seems to serve no purpose other than to thwart his plans, which means it's pointless. The offside rule seems to have been created to annoy the world: "Did you score a goal? Yes, but no… It's offside because there weren't *at least two players between you and the goal*!" And gnagnagna… There are plenty more rules like that to be made. Why not stipulate that at least three players must be in the centre circle at the time of the goal for it to be valid? Or that the goalkeeper opposite is drinking water, or that at least one of the players is called Patrick?

Obedience to the law we have prescribed for ourselves is freedom.

In fact, it's easy to delude yourself when you think you're free. As we've seen, we tend to confuse freedom with pleasure. But just because we act spontaneously doesn't mean we're free. The person who sleeps in may feel freer than the one who is dragged out of bed by his alarm clock. However, the reason why staying in bed is so pleasant is that we are subjected to the fatigue of our body, to which we are therefore enslaved. In the same way, a smoker may feel freer when he's in a place where he's not forbidden to smoke. Yet everyone will admit that they are addicted. It's the need to smoke that drives him and his nicotine fix that gives him so much pleasure. On the contrary, we'd say that we're all the freer when we find the will to quit: we give up the pleasure of smoking, it's not easy, and we feel we're doing everything in our power not to give in to temptation. But as we understand it, this feeling of effort that counteracts the desire to smoke is not opposed to freedom. On the contrary, it manifests the power of the will against desire. And as Rousseau would say, when we forbid someone to smoke, we're actually forcing them to be free. In the *Social Contract*, Rousseau says above all that obeying the rules in no way prevents one from being free, "for the impulse of appetite alone is slavery, and obedience to the law one has prescribed for oneself is freedom.[54]" In fact, it's important to realize that we're always subject to rules, even and especially when we ignore them. A person who sleeps when he's tired, eats when he's hungry or drinks when he's thirsty may well feel pleasure because he's satisfying a natural need. Yet he is subject to a law, that of his biological nature. This is what Rousseau calls "the impulse of appetite alone". We're used to wishing people "bon appétit", as if they had a choice. But appetite can't be decreed, and it's hardly possible to say that it's "good". Basically, it's just a sensation that manifests a need: hunger, thirst or sleep. And to act on the impulse of appetite is simply to be a slave to your body, which is

------

54. ROUSSEAU (Jean-Jacques), *Du contrat social,* liv. I, chap. VIII, GF-Flammarion, 1992, p. 44.

VII. Why are Women Incapable of Understanding Offside?

not a very glorious thing to do. The person who manages to restrain himself is undoubtedly freer. Even though I'm tired, I force myself to get up, and even though I'm ravenously hungry, I'll wait until mealtime to eat. That's why I feel forced, coerced or annoyed. But it's not my will that I'm thwarting; on the contrary, it's my natural tendencies that would like to enslave me to their law.

It's easy to see how feeling obliged by a rule doesn't prevent us from being free, but on the contrary sets us free. Rousseau speaks of "the law we have prescribed for ourselves". In fact, I'm not the one who set the laws of my biological nature: I have to eat and drink if I don't want to die, and that's not my fault. On the other hand, when I *force* myself to get up after programming my alarm clock, I'm complying with the law I've prescribed for myself; I'm acting in accordance with the rule I've given myself, which is to get up at 6 or 7 o'clock. When I sleep, I don't feel obliged, but I am a slave to my body. And when I get up, if I feel obliged, it's precisely because I'm fighting against this law of nature. And yet, when you obey the rules of a sport, you are all the more free to obey "the law you have prescribed for yourself". Nobody asked the footballer to be a footballer. Nobody asked him to engage in a game where you had to kick a ball into a goal. So he freely chose to abide by all the rules of the game. Why should he? That's his business. He undoubtedly sees pleasure and interest in it, particularly in showing himself to be stronger than the others in his ability to develop all the qualities needed to win: tactics, solidarity, stamina, and so on. From this point of view, it seems absurd to complain about the existence of these rules. Anyone who doesn't play soccer is under no obligation to respect offside, and if you do play, it's because you want to. No ?

The social contract

One imagines that the striker would be freer if there were no offside rule. But freedom from what? In the *Social Contract*, Rousseau asserts that we are much freer when we must obey laws, and we could say that a soccer player is freer when he is limited by the offside rule. Astonishing? In fact, "we must distinguish between natural freedom, which is limited only by the individual's own strength, and civil freedom[55]". Indeed, if there were no law or rule to restrict individual freedom, we would be totally free. But in the end, we wouldn't be free at all! This "natural freedom" wouldn't really be freedom at all, because individuals would have every right, including the right to kill or steal from their neighbors if they felt the need or inclination. You can imagine the result: society would obey the law of the strongest, and in the end, very few people would be free, or even feel free, always worried about what might fall in their lap. To avoid this situation, it would be in the interest of most people to make a contract with each other: "You don't kill me, I don't kill you". In this way, everyone

---

55. *Ibid*, p. 43-44.

agrees to abide by rules such as "thou shalt not kill", which are the same for everyone, allowing us to live more peacefully and protect the weakest. This is how we should view the relationship between soccer players. Admittedly, soccer is a sport of collective confrontation. But it's not about a fight where no holds are barred. It's not about pitting your natural physical strength against that of others, and you don't beat your opponent just because you hit him with a ball. Just as there seems to be a contract between members of society, there is also a contract between players. We all agree to play by the rules. The winner is the one who manages to put a goal past his opponent, having respected all the rules to which we have *all* agreed to submit in the *same way*. In this sense, soccer is supposed to show us how to be free, by teaching us that one person's freedom ends where another's begins. This is what we call "fair play".

The Oulipo

Strangely enough, some people don't consider rules to be part of the game, as if they were some kind of accident[56]. But playing soccer without rules would be like playing Scrabble, where you're allowed to make up words that don't

---

56. In fact, the famous refereeing disputes seem to be caused less by the offside rule itself than by the modifications made to weaken it. Indeed, it was probably when the striker was allowed to be on the *same line* as the last defender that the offside position was made much more difficult to see and define, both with the naked eye and on video.

exist in the dictionary. And as someone else would say: it's restrictive, but it makes the game a little more interesting. In fact, it's the rules that make the game exist. Imagine a sport with no rules at all: you wouldn't say you had to kick a ball into the opponent's goal, or that you had to play it with your feet. What kind of game would it be? It would be hard to tell, and the players themselves wouldn't even know what they were doing. And if we were to remove the rule that forbids playing the ball with the hand, we'd be talking about soule, the ancestor of soccer, where all shots are allowed. The game would then be reduced to a purely physical confrontation between two groups, a pitched battle—and still—violent, brutal and, to put it bluntly, masculine. Similarly, there might well be no offside rules, but that wouldn't really be soccer. Indeed, soccer is a team sport which, in addition to physical skills, undoubtedly enables the development of specific qualities such as *solidarity* and *tactical thinking*. However, it is the offside rule that forces footballers to play as a team. Without it, a striker would simply position himself in front of the opponent's goal, leaving his team-mates to go about *their* business and wait for the ball to arrive at his feet. The game would resemble a kind of giant volleyball, with players throwing the ball back and forth across the field with a flurry of clearances. No running, no dribbling, no confrontation and, in a word, no movement. Basically, the offside rule lives up to its name: a player *must not* take part in the game unless there are at least two players between him and the opposing goal. But it's a *fact* that you don't take part in the game if you prefer to stay on your own. Requiring the striker to be surrounded by two other players simply forces each player to play with the others in what must remain a team sport. If you have to be at least two in front of the goal, you can only score if you're united: you have to give the ball to each other and pass it back, gradually working *together* up to the opponent's goal.

If soccer players weren't restricted by the offside rule, they'd have no reason to develop *tactical thinking* and play systems. Tactics involve thinking about how to organize the movements of team members. It's the kind of game intelligence that we demand of our players, and through which they develop their intellectual qualities. However, if all you had to do was send the ball to an attacker standing in front of the opponent's goal, there'd probably be no tactics. Because there have to be at least two of us in front of the goal, we have to think about how we're going to get there. It's important to know whether you're playing in the middle or on the flanks, attacking in twos or threes, for the sole reason that you have to get to the goal by crossing the field. This would not be the case if the attacker could be offside. Here again, the name of the rule is welcome: without offside, there would be no game. To do without offside would be to deprive players of everything that forces them to play, think, create, invent—in short, to exploit and develop their sporting talents.

In 1969, Georges Perec wrote *La disparition*, a book that doesn't include the letter "E" once. Obviously, he did this on purpose. Why did he do it? Quite simply, the idea was to impose a rule on himself, a constraint that would force him to use his imagination[57]. It's easy to see that the handicap he gave himself forced him to make a certain amount of effort to come up with ideas that he probably wouldn't have thought of if he'd written "normally". If you start telling a story and you can't use words with an "E" in them, you'll have to come up with new ones, and in so doing, take paths you hadn't anticipated. In the end, we've undoubtedly created something unexpected. This is a lesson that could be given to all those who defend the idea of ethnic cleansing or more or less natural selection. Without going so far as to evoke the purity of the Aryan race, we can think of the dreams made possible by modern biology: avoiding abnormal children, choosing one's baby's eyes, and so on. However, it is thanks to the "accidents" of procreation that the human species is evolving. If we were to start making babies on a programmed basis, we'd be robbing human life of any chance of inventing new forms. It's only through abnormal individuals that species evolution is possible, and if Cro-Magnon man had always had normal children, we'd still be Cro-Magnon man.

That said, the world of soccer probably wouldn't be much different…

---

57. Georges Perec (1936-1982) was a member of the "Oulipo", Ouvroir de Littérature Potentielle, a literary and scientific group founded by poet Raymond Queneau in 1960. The Oulipo movement focused on the way in which constraint can influence creativity.

VIII. Is Zidane an Artist?
(Is Genius Subject to no Rules?)

"In pursuing their great interests, great men have often treated other inherently venerable interests, and even sacred rights, lightly and inconsiderately. This is a course of conduct that is certainly open to moral reproach. But their position is quite different. Such a great figure necessarily crushes many an innocent flower, ruins many a thing in its path."

G.W.F. Hegel

The genius of the headbutt

Zidane's headbutt was astonishing. It's not so much that the French international took a violent swipe at an opponent, given his public image as an introverted prodigal son. After all, he had already "wiped his feet" on a Saudi during a group match at the 1998 World Cup. It was then that he stood out from the crowd, becoming the first French player to receive a red card at a World Cup finals. Nor is it surprising that "Zizou" kicked the ball. After all, soccer is played "from head to foot", and you're entitled to make crude mistakes with either: the foot against the Saudi, the head against the Italian. No, what's really astonishing is the way the ball was struck on Materazzi's chest. In other words, Zidane is such a brilliant, unpredictable and extraordinary artist that even his headbutt is a work of art. Where did he get that upper body inclination? Usually, when you take a ball shot, the movement starts from the neck or, at best, from the shoulders. But Zidane doesn't do anything like everyone else, and it's undoubtedly the genius of his gesture, perfect both technically and physically, that explains the indulgence shown by most observers, starting with coach Raymond Domenech. "When *you take a shot* like he did for 1 hour 20 minutes and *the referee* just lets it go, you understand. You don't excuse it, but you understand." The poor kid, he "took it", even though we thought he was a very strong player, a genius, and so on. And as usual, it's the referee's fault. While we are still wondering whether Thierry Henry should not be tried at the International Criminal Tribunal in The Hague for high treason and undermining state security, we admit that we can understand Zidane. After all, the macaroni insulted his mother and sister! Fucking hell! Fucking wop!

You think that's rude? Well, that's more or less what the lyrics of a hit song from the summer of 2006 say: "Zidane il a tapé… le rital il a eu mal" ("Zidane typed… the wop hurt"). While everyone is crying foul about poor Thierry Henry, whose behavior is supposed to shame France, Zidane's headbutt is a hit. We love it. However, we have to admit that Zidane's behavior in 2006 was worse than Thierry Henry's at the 2010 World Cup. "Titi" merely committed a foul in the course of play; he used his hand without ever questioning the sovereignty of the referee and, above all, without harming anyone's physical integrity. His hand is a foul. Outside soccer, it would be a perfectly valid and regular gesture, for example in handball or rugby. And outside sport, it would be a gesture with no value, good or bad. No one has ever been arrested for touching a ball with their hand! On the other hand, Zidane's headbutt is not only forbidden in soccer, since it's supposed to teach morality, respect for the rules and for one's opponent, but it's also a gesture forbidden by the laws[58]. As a result, Zizou's gesture is far more detrimental to state security, insofar as it is one of the behaviors banned by the Republic as a minimum condition for living together. If everyone were allowed to engage in violent behavior, society would be ruined.

---

58. Article R624-1 of the French *Penal Code* punishes "intentional violence which has not resulted in total incapacity for work" with a fine of at least the amount stipulated for 4th class offences. It also provides for "confiscation of the thing that was used or intended to commit the offence, or of the thing that is the product of it". So it's Zizou's head rather than Henry's that we should be calling for!

Are great men above the law?

Basically, then, Zidane's behavior cannot be justified or excused at all, and it's hardly understandable. Even so! We're told "we understand". But we don't have to understand this kind of attitude coming from a soccer player! The many supporters Zidane has received explain that he was merely reacting to an unfair provocation. We even regret that it's always the reaction that is punished and not the provocation. But what is this two-euro defense? Isn't sport supposed to teach us self-control, respect for others and for ourselves? That it channels our violence and aggression? As we have seen[59], strength is not violence, and sportsmen and women are all the stronger for knowing how to play by the rules, demonstrating patience, concentration and so on. And now we're being told that "there are limits, aren't there? Boxers come to mind: paradoxically, this sport, which is all about punching each other in the face, teaches self-control. If you start by getting angry because someone throws you a right hook, it's hard to win. The idea behind boxing is undoubtedly that, despite suffering, you have to keep a cool head and continue to think about the placement of your punches, your guard, etc. As for the football player, if he's going to get hurt, he has to keep his head. As for the soccer player, if he's able to channel his strength and think about his leg placement

---

59. Cf. *Infra*, chap. V, *Team spirit*, "Strength is not violence".

in order to kick in the stride, why shouldn't he also be able to prevent himself from reacting to a "provocation"? It's contradictory, and all the more astonishing when we're talking about a player whom everyone admires for his *great* technical mastery, this and that.

Understandably, the justification has nothing to do with the seriousness of the act. Instead, we have to admit that this is one of the most violent acts ever committed by a player in this kind of competition, and is on a par with the assault on Battiston by German goalkeeper Schumacher in the 1982 World Cup semi-final. Apparently, there's a level of glory or genius that excuses everything. An abstract, hard-to-define line beyond which an individual's actions are at best worthless, at worst just another element in the figure of the idol. Maradona springs to mind: firstly, for his hand of God, whose name echoes the religious metaphor that characterizes "idols". Secondly, for his life as a drug addict, celebrated by Kusturica. This undoubtedly explains the difference in treatment between Zidane and Henry: one is a great player, the other just a good one; one is a genius, the other just talented; one is a god, the other just a man. A strange concept of moral values, blame and judgement, which grants indulgences to certain individuals for "sporting services rendered to the nation".

But it's not a question of sport. It's a very general cultural problem: there's a discrepancy, even a contradiction, between society's moral values and its cultural values. There are many examples of individuals more or less regarded as heroes whose more or less proven genius excuses everything. What, for a normal person, is a serious breach of morality becomes, in the case of an exceptional being, a joke, a whim that can be justified. And *Sophie's World* has nothing to envy to that of soccer. Martin Heidegger, for example, is a great German philosopher revered by a whole host of Heideggerians, who don't like it at all to be reminded that their god was a card-carrying member of the Nazi party. Another one? Louis Althusser, less well known to the general public. Read what BHL has to say about him—even if it's not a reference: "*Althusser* is a lighthouse. A lighthouse in the literal sense. In other words, an intense, brief, blinding light, but one that was short-lived. A spotlight emerging from the night and returning to it". Yes, a lighthouse! Ask his wife, he strangled her! But a BHL will tell you that he's "a possessed Dostoyevskian, who has reached the end of his night" Ah! pardon! My mistake! I hadn't understood. By the way, in the literary genre of "parvenu au bout de la nuit" (reached the end of the night), there's Céline, Louis Ferdinand by his sweet first name, whom Fabrice Luchini never stops quoting as if he were also the lighthouse of the human condition. But in *Bagatelle pour un massacre,* he wrote, among other things: "The 15 million Jews will fuck the 500 million Aryans." It's beautiful… I'm almost teary-eyed. In any case, the great writer has nothing to envy the PSG fans who are banned from stadiums for less, while Céline is being played at the theater, he who wrote: "Personally I find Hitler, Franco, Mussolini fabulously debonair, admirably magnanimous, infinitely too much in my opinion, bleating pacifists to say the least!" But as is the case with Heidegger, there are always people who explain that it's not fair to say he's anti-Semitic, even if it's true, because that's not all he was! But then, I'd also say that Hitler was very nice in private! "We got to know him best during the war." For example, we had to call him every day to give him news of his dog when he wasn't at his Berghof residence in Bavaria. And nobody was allowed to touch his beast. Didn't he respect the animal cause? An admiring critic wrote of *Bagatelle pour un massacre*: "In it, Céline deals with a multitude of themes revealing not only his time, but also the preoccupations dear to the writer. These include literature, alcohol and cinema, which Céline blamed for the decadence of French society in the late 1930s. Céline's pacifism is also evident in this text." Obviously! The pacifist who wants to fuck the Jews and who is right to talk about the decadence of the thirties. Where's the decadence of the thirties? It wouldn't be with the NAZIS, would it? What did he smoke? Speaking of smoking, I'm thinking of Baudelaire's *Les paradis artificiels* d'un mangeur d'opium. It's beautiful, it's Baudelaire. Yes, but it's opium! And Bertrand Cantat, who killed his girlfriend with his bare hands? Michael Jackson: paedophile; Roman Polansky: the same; Rimbaud: arms dealer; Verlaine: attempted murderer; Herbert von Karajan: Nazi. Every time, people say: "He's a great artist". If you did or said a quarter of a third of a tenth of the horrors committed by all these people, you'd be pilloried for eternity. Why would they do that? Because we men aren't great artists! If we can align two lines of verse, shoot a film, write a song, conduct an orchestra or dribble, we can kill the whole Earth. And in this respect, Hitler's greatest fault was perhaps not to have persevered in painting.

Art is the spirit of the people

Certainly, works of art and their creators are not and must not be subject to any moral or even legal rules. When you make a war film, you have every right to cover monuments with a Nazi flag; the characters can utter the worst atrocities. In general, the author of a book, film or play is not prosecuted for the speech he places in the mouths of his characters. According to Hegel, this is due to the specific function of art, whose aim is to express the spirit of an age: works of art are the mirror in which a society places its image of itself: what are its moral values, its laws, its relationship to its own history, its political ideal or its religion? "It is in works of art that peoples have deposited their richest intimate thoughts and representations, and often beautiful art is the only key by which we are given to penetrate the secrets of their wisdom and the mysteries of their religion.[60]" In short, art is the reflection of a culture—

---

60. HEGEL (Friedrich), *Esthétique*, t. I, introduction (trans. from German by C. Bénard, revised by B. Timmermans and P. Zaccaria), Le livre de poche, "Classiques de la philosophie", 1997, pp. 57-58.

Greek, medieval, capitalist, Western or Eastern—on itself. An entire people contemplates itself through its works of art, just as I see myself in the reflection of a mirror. This is undoubtedly why many works of art that bear witness to the present end up as historical documents, such as Zola's depiction of the nineteenth-century working class. Even science fiction isn't a hypothesis about the future; it's the way a culture represents its future: its fears, its hopes and its values. Jules Verne's *Paris in the 20th century* is not to be judged on the accuracy of his "forecasts" for the present. Rather, it tells us what was expected of the future, and how people felt about it at the end of the 19th century. Conversely, a historical film is not a report on the past: it's an expression of a society's relationship with its past. Think of American films about Vietnam, whose sheer number reveals the trauma of the war: "What were we going to do in that mess? The *Rambos* of the early '80s, on the other hand, try to show that we were right to take on these niakoués, even if we lost. So we invented a hero to console ourselves for the defeat of "this fucking war". But the second half of the 1980s saw the emergence of other kinds of films that revealed a different vision of America: *Platoon* and *Full Metal Jacket*. Here, it's the absurdity and illegitimacy of Vietnam that are reflected upon, and Rambo is no longer a box-office hit.

So we understand that censorship cannot be applied to works of art and artists: it would be like forbidding a historian to read documents because they're not pretty to look at. It would be as if the doctor forbade his patient to talk about his sexual practices because they were dirty; as if the priest refused to hear the penitent's confession because it was wrong; as if the lawyer didn't want to know about his client's life because he had committed reprehensible acts. A people that forbids itself to produce works of art is like one that turns away from mirrors, and refuses to see its reality in the face. That said, the fact that the artist is free in his works does not mean that he has every right as a man or in civil life, so to speak. What then? If we take up Hegel's idea of the great men of history, we could say that it is the great visions of these artists that justify our willingness to overlook their infringements of the law and morality[61]. To reach their lofty heights, they have to break free of the rules to which ordinary people are bound. The artist must undoubtedly step outside his or her own culture, if he or she is to look at it from a different angle.

But what does this have to do with Zidane? You might ask. Well, that's precisely the question I'm asking myself. I'm not the one saying that Zidane is an artist!

---

61. "But right is on their side because they are lucid: they know what the truth of their world and their time is… but a right of a particular kind" (HEGEL (Friedrich), *Reason in History*, trans. from the German by K. Papaioannou, 10/18, "Les grands hommes", 1993).

Is the footballer an artist?

I remember the famous quarter-final between France and Brazil at the 2006 World Cup. It was referred to as the French team's "masterpiece", and Zidane's "performance" was undoubtedly what people had in mind. In terms of goals, it was just a 1-0 scoreline for France. But it has to be said that this single goal alone symbolized the extraordinary performance of the French players: constant control and possession of the ball, with the Brazilians incapable of finding a solution. I especially remember Zidane in midfield, spending his time distributing the ball to his teammates to move it towards the opposition goal. I remember his dribbling, footwork, footwork, one-twos and roll-outs. What Ronaldinho could only do in a commercial, Zidane did in a World Cup quarter-final. In particular, he left Cafu, the Brazilian team's regular defender and captain, on the spot with a series of *feints*: he launched a shot with the outside of his right foot, before blocking the ball with the sole of his foot; he hooked the ball inwards and rolled it to his left foot, to make an outside pass. 2 seconds, watch in hand! It's easy to think of it as inspiration. But is that enough to say that a soccer player is an artist?

Admittedly, the term is used in all sorts of ways. Personally, when people talk to me about artists, I tend to think of Picasso, Mozart or De Niro. At first glance, there are no artists except in art, which defines itself as a certain category of *craft*. There are politicians, teachers, lawyers, doctors, bakers and artists. The artist is the one who creates a more or less material object. He manufactures an object in such a way that one might say: "It's quite an art". The painter knows how to draw, the musician how to play his instrument. However, we know that the craftsman also has a skill, but we wouldn't say that he's an artist. The difference is that the artist doesn't produce something useful. The artisan baker makes bread for eating, the shoemaker makes shoes for walking. But why does the musician or painter produce his work? For nothing, except to be contemplated, looked at and listened to, which is not at all necessary, as the expression "You might as well be pissing on a violin" suggests. Take soccer shirts, for example. We all know that the primary function of their colors is to distinguish the two teams on the pitch, so much so that we end up associating them with their team: the "Sang et Or" of Lens, the "Verts" of Saint-Étienne, "les Bleus" or the Italian "Squadra azura". Indeed, when France meets Italy, one of the two teams has to give up its blue so that spectators can distinguish their respective teams. Here, the color is purely utilitarian. On the other hand, we also know that for some time now, people have been trying to ensure that jerseys look good and are not just identifiable: the Italians, in particular, have adopted a kind of tight-fitting jersey with a tight collar. Here, we go beyond the consideration of utility. In the same way, artists invent beautiful things.

But is soccer an art? Perhaps it is. Admittedly, it's first and foremost a sport whose aim is to maintain the body and even the mind, for all the reasons we know: "Anima Sana In Corpore Sanum", as the ASICS sports brand puts it. But this doesn't rule out artistic forms of expression. Indeed, there's nothing to stop soccer players from performing gestures and movements that are not only useful, but also beautiful to look at. This is what makes an artist: playing "for the beauty of the gesture", the touch of the ball, the passing of the legs, the dribble that is judged not by its efficiency, but by its beauty. Indeed, many of the activities classified as "sports" and recognized as Olympic disciplines have an essentially aesthetic aim. Such is the case with gymnastics, diving, figure skating, freestyle skiing, etc., and this is the problem with these "sports", which often give rise to controversy, since victory rests on the appreciation of judges, whose tastes can be as relative and debatable as those of art and film critics. Moreover, there are classical arts whose sole aim is to express the beauty of bodily movement, in particular dance, not to mention the *happenings* and other performances that are multiplying in modern and so-called *underground* artistic expression. It could even be argued that modern art, where we end up finding just about anything and everything, has far less merit than the works of footballers. Personally, I'm less reluctant to say that Zidane's leg-swings are a work of art than I am to grant that title to works such as "merde d'artiste" by the Italian Piero Manzoni, who exhibits his poo. By what criteria would Manzoni be more of an artist than his soccer-playing compatriots? Ultimately, then, there's really no reason to deny footballers the title of artist, especially as the boundaries of art are pretty blurry.

Is the footballer a genius?

The problem is that the term "artist" is associated with a number of ideas that are quite contrary to the spirit of sport in general and soccer in particular. When we think of the artist, we think of a genius inspired by an almost divine breath, with exceptional qualities. Mozart's contemporaries report that his manuscripts were free of erasures, meaning that his writing was spontaneous and the fruit of immediate inspiration. In fact, he spent much of his time tapping away at anything he could get his hands on, as if he were constantly hearing voices and music. The artist seems to have been endowed with innate, natural or even supernatural faculties, which alone explain his skill. How did Michelangelo manage to paint the ceiling of the Sistine Chapel? In other words, we don't know how he did it, or where he got it all from. And it's probably in the same sense that we speak of an artist or a genius when we describe the gestures and performances of a soccer player like Zidane. Only he can do that, because he has a unique gift, so much so that since his retirement, people have been looking for the "new Zidane". This pointless question shows that Zizou's performances are not seen as the fruit of the work and effort that any conscientious player could produce. And if some players are expensive or worth millions, it's for exactly the same reason. As in the legend of *Excalibur,* where only he who is destined to be king will be able to remove the sword from its rock, we must first find the chosen one.

The problem is that this image of the great player is so contrary to the spirit of the sport that the heroes produced by show soccer seem to be killing off sporting values. Afterwards, it's claimed that top-level sport encourages the practice of mass sport, but I think it's just the opposite. "Talent" is often used to describe the best soccer players. This means that the player in question has a natural ability—to play, to dribble, to read the game—that has nothing to do with training or hard work. Or rather, talent would be a natural disposition specially adapted to perform all the gestures that soccer requires mastery of. All this leads to the disappearance of the boundary between the innate and the acquired, which is very contrary to the spirit of sport. Firstly, it will no longer be possible to claim that top-level sport is a social elevator that enables "young people" to "get by". If professional soccer is reserved for a bunch of geniuses, it's hard to see how it would be useful to start working to learn to play soccer—since it can't be learned. It's also contrary to the ideas of hard work, discipline and effort that are so essential to the sport. Ironically, professional footballers don't at all offer the model of success—sporting, social or economic—through hard work: as the idea that they are artists or geniuses is left to linger, they show instead that it's not very complicated to succeed in life. It's the model of ease that they offer: no need to work, talent is enough.

German realism and Brazilian samba

On the contrary, there's a tendency to devalue the so-called "hard-working" player as always embodied by the German, no doubt in remembrance of the Third Reich. Thus, poor Lothar Matthaüs, eternal captain of the "Mannschaft"—so named as a reminder of the "Wehrmacht"—is presented as the eternal player who masters the rules perfectly and often wins, without dazzling anyone. Even when awarding him the Ballon d'Or in 1990, the editors of *France Football* were almost apologetic: "Matthäus, if he isn*'t Pelé* […]. Matthäus, apart from having exceptional vital energy and a real taste for commitment and contact, is a footballer *of rule and conscience.* Individually, he's not *sublime in any way*; but he's *good in every expression of the game* and quite remarkable in the use of his ball-striking.[62]" *He's not sublime in any way.* Nice! He's the captain, the fulcrum of his team and the man who wins every other World Cup for Germany, but he's not sublime! In other words, you can always work hard, win all the competitions and even the Golden Ball, but you'll never be a great player anyway, because you're not an artist! At the other end of the spectrum, of course, are the *seleçao's* natural-born players, who are just as clichéd. In FIFA's own words, "the 1970 edition in Mexico will forever be remembered for the *dazzling performances* of Brazilian *artists*". Here we find

---

62. THIBERT (Jacques), *France Football*, no. 2333, December 25 1990.

the "sublime" that was lost in Matthaüs' feet: "dazzling" performances. The Brazilians' performances therefore seem to be produced by players who have soccer in their blood, so that they constitute a species particularly born for soccer. But I'd like someone to explain to me what the soccer gene looks like, and whether we can really believe that Nature, in its immense wisdom, planned to choose a chosen people for this sport. Our prejudices lead us to mix things up a bit: since there's Carnival in Rio, we imagine that Brazilian footballers play soccer like they dance. And since the Germans led the war against the Allies, they are eternal soldiers obeying orders.

In fact, it could be argued that Matthaüs is no more devoid of talent than the Brazilians are artists. What everyone forgets, even when talking about Zidane, is that mastering a sport takes work. It's all very well to admire a player's technique and, as in the case of Zidane, the precision and speed of his leg-spinning. But he has had to work and train to achieve the apparent ease that only comes from years of effort. As anyone who plays a musical instrument, or even drives a car, knows: it takes a lot of practice, hard work and self-discipline to be able to execute these gestures without thinking about them. And anyone who has never played the piano realizes just how handicapped you are at the keyboard when you've learned nothing. Work, erased by work. It's the discipline that enables the body to adopt movements that don't come naturally to anyone. "It is in this way," writes Nietzsche, "that our vanity, our self-love, encourages the cult of genius: for it is only on condition that it is supposed to be very distant from us, like a *miraculum*, that it does not hurt us [...]. All human activity is complicated by miracles, not only that of genius: but none of it is a miracle.[63]"

Individualism or the collective?

Soccer would be won by the descent of a son of God to give the good word and distribute the right balls. And after the crucifixion of the messiah, nailed to the pillory because of his own headbutt, we await the advent of a new prophet. But where is the next Zidane? Benzema, perhaps? Once again, soccer as a spectacle is rotting and overturning the values of sport: team spirit in favor of *individualism*[64]. As a result, we tend to believe that the

---

63. NIETZSCHE (Friedrich), *Humain, trop humain*, part I, chap. IV, 162 (trans. from the German by A.-M. Desrousseaux and H. Albert, revised by A. Kremer-Marietti). Albert, revised by A. Kremer-Marietti), Le livre de poche, "Classiques de la philosophie", 1995, p. 157.

64. The appalling results of *France Football's Ballon d'Or awards* reinforce this image, which runs counter to team spirit. The aim is to reward the "best player" of the year, first in Europe until 2006, and since then in the world. I've done my sums for the winners from 1989-2009: out of twenty-one Ballon d'Or winners, thirteen are strikers and five are midfielders who clearly owe their prize to the goals they scored (Matthäus, Baggio, Zidane, Rivaldo, Figo). In all, eighteen golden balls out of twenty-one were awarded to strikers and other types of attackers. The only real midfielders or defenders to be rewarded in twenty years are three: Sammer, Nedved and Cannavaro. It's hard to find the philosophy of team sport in this prize-giving, which could well be awarded to mussels who wait quietly by the goal for the ball to fall into their laps.

outcome of a match depends solely on a providential man, God, hero or Messiah. A journalist asks: "By the way, what was the French team like without Zizou, before his debut on August 17, 1994 against the Czechs, a match in which he scored two goals?[65]" And without Zidane? What about the other players? Don't they exist? The team doesn't exist? Doesn't the team exist?

After that, it's hardly surprising that the players themselves, Zizou first and foremost, are prepared to ruin their team's chances to settle personal scores on the pitch. In any case, "l'équipe de France, c'est moi!"

---

65. MARINO (Philippe), *L'express*, June 23, 2006. The article continues: "At the time, France only had Euro 1984 to their name, and had an eternal reputation on the footballing planet as a team capable of great things but rarely able to go all the way. Since Zizou's two goals in the 1998 final, France have become accustomed to winning. And Zizou has become a sort of talisman: if he's there, everything's fine, no matter what else is going on. And, inevitably, when he's not there, France is afraid, as Roger Gicquel would say. To the point of begging him to come back, after his false departure in 2004." And once again we find the "German realism" and the "Brazilian genius".

"Yes I know my enemies
They're the teachers who taught me to fight me
Compromise, conformity, assimilation, submission
Ignorance, hypocrisy, brutality, the elite
All of which are amrican dreams."[66]

66. "Yes, I know my enemies, they are the teachers who taught me *to* fight against myself, compromise, conformism, assimilation, submission, ignorance, hypocrisy, brutality, the elites, everything that belongs to the American dream", *Rage against the machine*, Sony Music Entertainement Inc., 1992.

Match sheet

I. Would Thierry Henry have been Better
off Playing Handball?
(Does the End Justify the Means?) 11

II. Why Say, "We Won,"
When we weren't Even on the Field?
(Is Soccer the Opium of the People?) 27

III. Would the Result of the Match
have been the Same if I Hadn't Watched It?
(Destiny and freedom) 45

IV. Can the Fans be Saved?
(Is Soccer the Nation's Last Refuge?) 61

V. "Team Spirit." Do Players only have
One Brain among Them?
(What are the Values of Sport?) 81

VI. Does the Referee get Paid?
(What is Justice?) 97

VII. Why are Women Incapable
of Understanding *Offside*?
(Does being Free mean Obeying no Rules?) 111

VIII. Is Zidane an Artist?
(Is Genius Subject to no Rules?) 127

Best sellers Max Milo Editions

Hitler's banker, Jean-François Bouchard

Confessions of a forger, Éric Piedoie Le Tiec

The Koran and the flesh, Ludovic-Mohamed Zahed

Governing by fake news, Jacques Baud

Governing by chaos, Lucien Cerise

A political history of food, Paul Ariès

Mad in U.S.A.: The ravages of the "American model", Michel Desmurget

Mondial soccer club geopolitics, Kévin Veyssière

Putin: Game master?, Jacques Baud

Treatise on the three impostors: Moses, Jesus, Muhammad, The Spirit of Spinoza

TV Lobotomy, Michel Desmurget

www.ingramcontent.com/pod-product-compliance
Lightning Source LLC
LaVergne TN
LVHW051158060726
842526LV00014B/3257